Roast Dinner

Roast Dinner

Delicious recipes for oven-cooked meals

Reader's Digest

Contents

Perfect roasting

Minimal effort, simple preparation, succulent flavours – these are just a few of the reasons why roasting is so popular. For results that are always tender and tasty, follow our useful guidelines.

Roasting

Roasting is a straightforward method for cooking meat – the joint or cut is simply cooked, uncovered in the oven, relatively slowly. Roasting may be a slow-cooking method, but the preparation is often quick and easy. And once the roast is in the oven, it needs only minimal attention.

Pot roasting

In the case of pot roasts, the meat is browned, then cooked slowly with a little liquid, often along with vegetables, until it is fork-tender. Technically, this is braising. The process requires time but not much attention.

Cooked to perfection

One of the tricks to roasting is to choose the right cuts, which should be reasonably tender, and to prevent them drying out so they remain moist and succulent. Here are some simple guidelines.

- To help keep a boned joint in a good shape and make sure it cooks evenly, tie it with string.
- Place the meat on a rack in a roasting pan so that the largest cut surfaces are exposed and any fat is on the top. As the fat melts during roasting it will baste the meat.
- If the meat is very lean, baste it with the hot fat in the roasting pan from time to time during cooking. Alternatively, cover the joint with foil.

Checking for doneness

Once the roasting time is completed, it can be difficult to judge if the meat is actually cooked – the outside may look perfect and deliciously browned, but the inside might still be a bit under-cooked. The most accurate test for doneness is by checking the internal temperature with a meat thermometer. Always make sure that the point of the thermometer goes into a thick part of the meat, not into fat or next to bone. To check poultry for doneness, insert a thin metal skewer into the thigh joint; the juices should run clear.

The best cuts for roasting

Beef:

Rib eye (scotch fillet), rump, sirloin, fillet (tenderloin), blade, topside, round, standing rib roast, rolled rib roast.

Lamb:

Leg (bone-in), shoulder (bone-in), easy carve (leg or shoulder), topside (round) roasts, boned and rolled loin, rump roast.

Roasting tips

Before cooking

Take the roast from the refrigerator about 15 minutes before cooking so that it reaches room temperature. Leave the meat, covered, in a cool place away from direct sun.

Choosing a pan

Use a roasting pan that is close to the size of the roast you are cooking. Leave space for root vegetables if cooking in the same dish.

Searing the meat

Recipes vary but generally, if a crust is desired, the outside of the meat is seared in a hot oven at 220°C (425°F/Gas 7) for about 20 minutes; the heat is then lowered to about 180°C (350°F/Gas 4) for the rest of the cooking time.

Slow-roasting

Timing and temperatures may vary slightly with individual recipes but for moist results without a crispy outside, the meat is generally cooked at a lower temperature of about 160°C (320°F/Gas 2–3) for the whole cooking time.

Resting

Always allow the roast to rest before carving. When a roast is removed from the oven, it needs to rest for 15–20 minutes. This allows the juices to settle and to be reabsorbed into the meat, which makes it easier to carve. While the meat rests, it will continue to cook and its internal temperature will rise 5–10 degrees.

Serving

Use a sharp knife to carve. To ensure a more tender slice, cut the meat across the grain. Arrange on a warmed serving platter or on individual plates.

Deglazing and making gravy

To deglaze the pan after roasting, remove the excess fat, then place the pan over high heat on the stove. Add liquid, such as water, stock or wine, and bring to a simmer. Scrape the bottom of the pan to loosen any stuck-on bits. Cook until the liquid is reduced, then strain and serve with the roast.

To make gravy, pour off all but 2 tablespoons of the fat from the pan, add 2 tablespoons plain (all-purpose) flour and stir over medium heat until browned. Pour in 2 cups (500 ml/16 fl oz) liquid, such as water or stock, and stir until smooth. Season with salt and pepper and pour into a sauce jug or gravy boat.

SIZING UP POULTRY

Judging how big a bird to buy depends on how many people you want to serve.

1.35–2.25 kg (3-5 lb)	serves	4–6
2.25–3.2 kg (5–7 lb)	serves	6–9
3.6–4 kg (8–9 lb)	serves	10–11
4.5–5 kg (10–11 lb)	serves	12–14
5.4–6 kg (12–13 lb)	serves	16–18
6.2–7.6 kg (14–17 lb)	serves	20–24
8–9 kg (18–20 lb)	serves	26–30

Roasting times

The cooking time for roasting meat is based on the weight of the joint, so weigh the meat and then calculate the cooking time according to the charts below. Individual recipes may vary but generally the ideal temperature for roasting is 180°C (350°F/Gas 4).

ROASTING CHART

Individual recipes may vary but these are ballpark roasting times. The times given are suitable for meat on or off the bone.

BEEF AND LAMB

Rare	20 mins per 500 g (1 lb) plus 20 minutes
Medium	25 mins per 500 g (1 lb) plus 25 minutes
Well-done	30 mins per 500 g (1 lb) plus 30 minutes

VEAL

Well-done	30 mins per 500 g (1 lb) plus 30 minutes

PORK

Medium	30 mins per 500 g (1 lb) plus 30 minutes
Well-done	35 mins per 500 g (1 lb) plus 35 minutes

CHICKEN

The rule of thumb for perfect roast chicken is 20 minutes per 500 g (1 lb), at a constant low temperature.

SLOW-COOKING ROASTING CHART

For slow roasting lamb, place meat in a 165°C (325°F/Gas 3) oven.

CUT		Minutes per 500 g (1 lb)
Whole leg, bone in	medium-rare	20
	medium	25
Boneless rolled whole leg	medium-rare	30
	medium	32–34
Leg, shank half, bone in	medium-rare	35–40
	medium	40–45
Leg, sirloin half, bone in	medium-rare	30–35
	medium	35–40

Basic equipment

Roasting pan Roasting pans and baking dishes come in a range of materials, including stainless steel, enamel and toughened glass.

Roasting rack Roasting racks elevate the meat from the fat that collects in the roasting pan during cooking.

Carving board A thick wooden board is best. Some designs have a groove around the edge to catch the meat juices.

Carving knife, fork, steel Your carving knife must be sharp and slightly flexible. Keep a steel handy to sharpen and hone the knife's edge. A carving fork will hold the meat in place while carving. Some forks have a guard to protect the hand while carving.

Glazing brush Used for greasing pans and basting meats and poultry with oil or pan juices while cooking. Look for a good-quality brush that will keep its bristles.

String Called cooking string or kitchen string, a roll of unbleached twine can be used to truss (tie) meats and poultry before roasting. Wet it to prevent stretching during cooking.

Thermometer A probe thermometer registers the slow rise of a roast's interior temperature during cooking. An instant-read thermometer is used near the end of cooking, outside the oven. It registers the temperature within seconds.

Carving

There's nothing quite like the joy of carving an aromatic roast at the dinner table. These tips and techniques will help ensure it all goes smoothly and your roast is carved to perfection.

An essential requirement for carving is a large razor-sharp knife and a carving fork. Some forks have a guard to prevent the knife slipping.

If the meat has been boned first, carving is easy, whatever the joint. You can simply cut the slices in the thickness you prefer, moving across the grain of the meat.

If the meat is on the bone, you will need to adjust your carving techniques accordingly. Here are a variety of common carving tasks with details about how best to proceed.

Carving boards and plates

You can use either a board or a plate as long as it is large enough and sits firmly on a surface that is non-slip. The plate or platter should be almost flat, as carving in a deep dish is virtually impossible.

If the table is slippery and the serving plate is made of china, put a cloth mat or folded napkin underneath to stop the dish from moving. And while it may look attractive to arrange the potatoes and other vegetables around the joint, this can make carving awkward and messy.

Rules for carving

For regular, attractive slices, make sure that the cuts go across the grain of the meat. Cutting with the grain tends to result in slices that are shredded and stringy. However, when carving undersides of joints like sirloin of beef or leg of lamb, it is easier to cut more thickly and with the grain of the meat.

Cold meat is generally sliced thinner than hot meat. If you are intending to serve the meat cold, wait until the joint cools before carving or the slices will lose their juices, colour and texture and won't be as appetising. It is also much easier to carve a cold joint.

Relaxed meat

Whatever meat you have roasted, take it out of the oven and leave it to stand for about 15–30 minutes, depending on its size, before it is carved.

Cover the joint with foil and put it in a warm place. Resting allows the juices to sink back from the surface of the roast and they can then be reabsorbed to moisten the meat. It also makes meat easier to carve, as juices will not spurt out.

Power carving

Electric carving knives are labour-saving if you have large amounts of meat to carve. However, they can be unwieldy and noisy and are not very suitable for use at the table. Also, it can be difficult to achieve very thin slices with an electric knife, especially when carving hot meat. Great care must be taken as electric knives are very sharp and can be dangerous to use.

Carving poultry

When carving small poultry, use a short, flexible carving knife and a table fork or small carving fork. It is much easier to carve chicken at the table if the wishbone is removed before the bird has been cooked. The method is quite simple: pull back the skin at the neck end to expose the breastbone, then cut and scrape with a short, sharp knife to extract the wishbone. Do not cut too deeply into the meat as you work. After the bone has been removed, tuck the skin back under the bird.

Cook's tip

If you want to avoid unattractive holes in your poultry when carving, turn the fork over. With practice, you will find that you can hold the bird securely with the back of the prongs without making marks in the meat.

Carving a large rib of beef

Cooking a rib of beef on the bone helps to conduct heat to the centre of a joint and gives a rich flavour. You can remove all the meat from the bone in one chunk and then carve it, but this rather spoils the effect. Try this way instead.

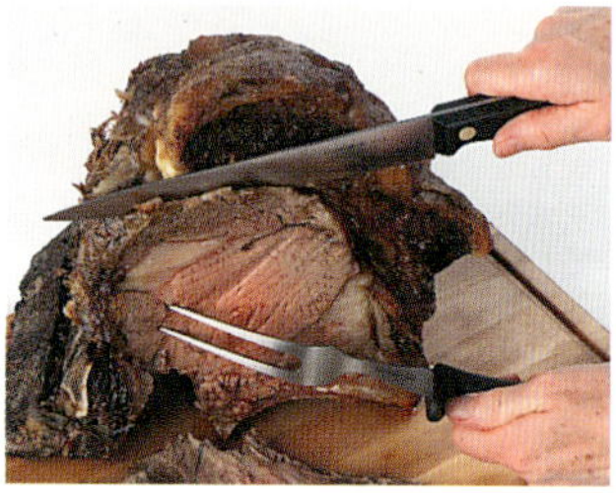

1 Place the rib of beef on its side and start by making a 5 cm (2 inch) deep cut along the ribs.

2 Stand the meat up, rib side down. Carve several slices, lift these off and place them on a warm dish.

3 Turn the rib back on its side and make a second 5 cm (2 inch) cut. Then stand the joint up and carve more.

Carving a shoulder of lamb

A shoulder can be quite tricky to carve because of the arched bone that runs through it. The secret is to carve it with the bone away from you, so you can get at the meat.

Put the shoulder skin side up and cut a long slice from the centre, on the side opposite the bone. Carve out more thick slices on either side, then horizontal slices from the top over the central bone. Turn the joint over and carve horizontally.

Carving a leg of lamb

Legs of lamb, pork and veal should all be carved in the same manner. The pictures below show the method used on a leg of lamb.

1 Put the leg meaty side up and cut a shallow 'V' from the middle. Carve slices downwards from both sides of the 'V', then turn the leg over and slice the rest horizontally.

2 Legs can also be cut in diagonal slices starting from the knuckle end. While this is most common with hams, the technique is an alternative you can try with all legs of meat.

Carving a loin roast

You can carve saddle of lamb by removing the loins from either side of the backbone and cutting across the grain. Alternatively, carve it on the bone as shown here.

1 The chump end of the saddle should be carved into thin slices across the grain of the meat, and at right angles to the backbone.

2 The main part of the saddle, lying each side of the backbone, is cut into thin strips or narrow slices down its full length.

Carving pork

Loins of lamb, pork and veal are all roasted on the bone to prevent shrinkage and preserve the flavour. But when you are ready to carve, it is easier to remove the meat from the rib cage and then slice it to the desired thickness. Pork is shown below.

1 Cut down between the chine bone and the meat and then angle the knife between the meat and the ribs, cutting the meat free of the bones. Remove the crackling from the joint in one piece.

2 The meat can now be sliced, and the crackling can be cut with scissors into the same number of pieces as there are slices of meat.

Cook's tip

To prevent cooked ham from discolouring or drying out, wrap it closely in plastic wrap. Joints will keep for up to 10 days in the refrigerator, but slices should be eaten within a few days. Alternatively, wrap the ham in a calico ham bag, previously rinsed in cold water and wrung out. Store in the refrigerator.

Carving a ham

Because a ham is so large, you need a special long, slim ham knife with a rounded tip to carve it properly. Make sure that it is razor sharp.

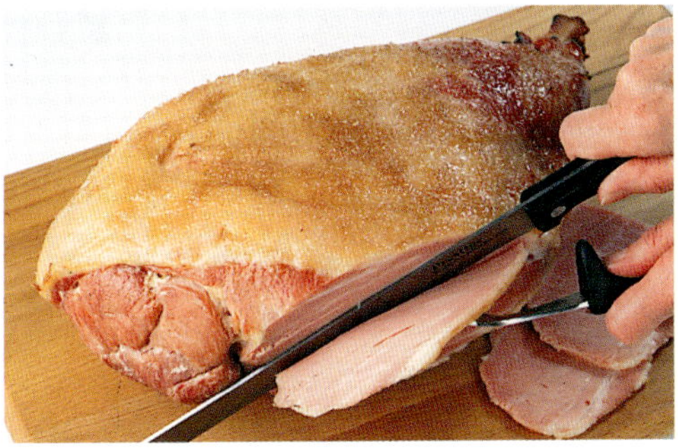

1 With the ham lying flat, fat side up, on a board and the knuckle bone pointing towards you, cut even slices along the side of the ham, parallel to the main bone of the leg, using a ham carving knife and fork.

2 After cutting a few slices, you will meet resistance from a small bone located near the knuckle end. Remove this bone with a small pointed knife, then continue cutting slices until you almost reach the main bone.

3 With the ham still lying flat on the board, cut slices from the large end of the ham – the end opposite the knuckle bone. Continue cutting slices in this direction until the leg's ball and cartilage are fully exposed.

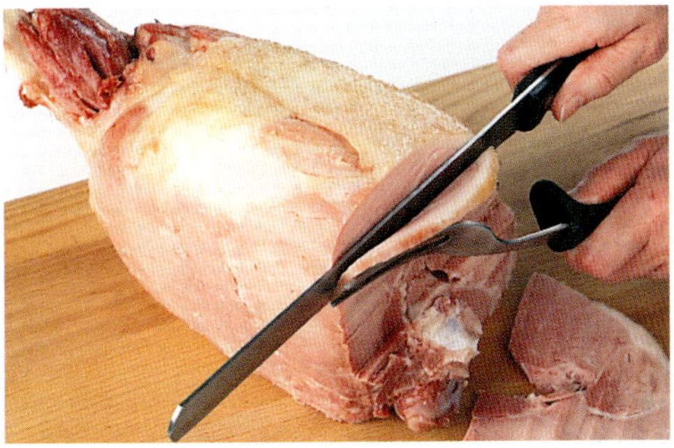

4 Stand the ham on its cut side and slice vertically towards the bone, then horizontally along the bone to release the slices. Grasp the knuckle and trim off the remaining meat by cutting parallel to the main bone.

Carving poultry

A chicken, duck, goose and small turkey are all carved in the same manner. For small birds, it is sometimes easier to remove the breast in one piece, as on this small chicken.

1 Place the bird on its side and cut under the thigh, lifting the whole leg up with a fork. To halve the leg, cut through the joint at the top of the drumstick.

2 Turn the bird breast side up. Cut down the breast, through the shoulder, and remove the wing, shoulder and breast in one piece.

3 If the bird is small, cut away the breast in one piece. If it is large, carve the breast into slices by starting at the wing end. Work your way towards the back and around to remove the shoulder, wing and a long strip of breast all in one piece. Lift this piece with the fork, holding the body down with the knife, and cut away.

Carving turkey

If a turkey weighs more than 5 kg (10 lb), put it on a board and carve it while it is firmly in place, as shown.

1 Remove the trussing string and then cut between the body and the thigh all around. Then cut through the connecting sinews.

2 Pull the leg away from the body and you can then carve the flesh into very small slices that are slanted parallel to the bone.

3 Cut down through the shoulder joint, removing breast meat attached to the shoulder and wing. Turn the bird and cut away the shoulder and wing on the other side in the same manner. This now clears the way for slicing the breast. A turkey breast is large enough to carve into slices on the bone.

Other techniques

Techniques such as stuffing and wrapping enhance roasted meats, poultry and fish. Tying or trussing a bird helps it keep its shape and stay moist while in the oven.

Stuffing and trussing a chicken

Small chickens can be prepared by simply tying the openings closed with a single piece of string, as shown. Large chickens must be trussed, the opening laced closed with string.

1 Remove the wishbone: with a sharp knife, cut through the flesh along the contours of the bone and lift it out.

2 Stuff the chicken loosely through the vent and neck cavities. Stuffing expands as it cooks, so don't pack it in.

3 Turn the bird on its back with the string beneath its tail. Pull the two ends up and cross them above the tail. Loop the ends over the drumsticks and draw to pull the legs over the vent.

4 Turn the bird over. Draw one string end over the thigh and around the upper wing. Repeat on the other side. Fold up the neck flap and firmly tie the two string ends over it.

Cook's tip

To truss a large chicken or turkey, first stuff the neck and body cavities. Secure the neck skin to the back with toothpicks or trussing pins.

Close the vent (opening of the cavity) with a skewer, toothpicks or trussing pins.

Tie the legs together securely over the vent with string. Insert a meat thermometer, if using. To protect the wing tips from burning, tuck them securely behind the shoulders.

Filling and rolling a chicken

It takes only a minute or two to fill, roll and secure each breast half. Take care not to overfill or roll too tightly or the chicken breast might split as it cooks.

1 Lay out the pounded breast halves with the short side facing you.

2 Spoon 2–3 tablespoons of stuffing onto each breast.

3 Starting at the short end, roll the meat gently, keeping the stuffing tucked in.

4 Secure with toothpicks, season with salt and pepper, and arrange in a baking dish.

Wrapping a fish parcel

This method of cooking is called *en papillote*, meaning 'in a paper casing'. The fish and seasonings bake in their own juices sealed inside the packet. The technique allows steam to assist in the cooking.

You can use baking paper or foil for the parcels. They can be assembled and refrigerated a few hours ahead. Remove them from the refrigerator ½ hour before baking.

1 Place the fish and vegetables to one side of the centre of baking paper or foil.

2 Fold the paper in half, then roll and press sides to close firmly.

3 Roll and press the lower edges towards the top opening of the parcel.

4 Fully enclose the parcel by rolling and pressing along the top opening, sealing firmly.

Meat

Sunday special roast beef

Succulent roast beef, crispy roast potatoes and root vegetables, and lovely feather-light Yorkshire puddings make one of the best loved of Sunday lunches. This healthy version will please everyone, even the traditionalists.

- 1.5 kg (3 lb) boned, rolled and tied lean sirloin of beef, trimmed of fat
- freshly ground black pepper
- 4 teaspoons English mustard (optional)
- 1.5 kg (3 lb) potatoes, peeled and cut into even-sized pieces
- 500 g (1 lb) baby parsnips
- 500 g (1 lb) baby carrots
- 3 tablespoons sunflower oil
- 1 kg (2 lb) broccoli florets
- 2 cups (500 ml/16 fl oz) beef stock

YORKSHIRE PUDDINGS

- ⅓ cup (50 g/1¾ oz) plain (all-purpose) flour
- salt
- 1 egg
- 100 ml (3½ fl oz) milk
- 2 teaspoons sunflower oil

Serves 8
Preparation 20 minutes
Cooking 2–2½ hours

1 Preheat the oven to 180°C (350°F/Gas 4). Put the meat, fat side up, on a rack in a roasting pan. Season with pepper, then spread with 3 teaspoons of the mustard, if using. Roast the meat in the oven according to the weight, basting occasionally with the juices in the pan.

2 Meanwhile, prepare the Yorkshire pudding batter. In a bowl, mix together the flour and a pinch of salt. Make a well in the centre and add the egg. Add a little of the milk and beat together, gradually beginning to work in the flour. Slowly beat in the remaining milk and 4 tablespoons water, until flour is incorporated and the batter is smooth. Set aside.

3 Next prepare the vegetables. Put the potatoes in a large saucepan of boiling water and boil for 5 minutes. Drain well and return to the pan, then cover and shake vigorously to roughen the surface of the potatoes (this helps to make them crisp). Cut the parsnips and carrots in half lengthwise and place in another large saucepan of boiling water and boil for 3 minutes, then drain.

4 One hour before the end of the roasting time for the beef, put 2 tablespoons of the oil in a non-stick roasting pan and the remaining 1 tablespoon oil in another non-stick roasting pan. Heat on top of the stove, then add the potatoes to the 2 tablespoons oil and the parsnips and carrots to the 1 tablespoon oil. Baste each piece of vegetable with oil, then quickly place the pans in the oven with the beef. After 30 minutes, turn the potatoes and vegetables so they will crisp and brown evenly.

5 When the beef is cooked, remove it from the oven and increase the heat to 220°C (425°F/Gas 7). Place the beef on a warmed plate, cover with foil to keep warm and allow to rest. Divide the oil for the Yorkshire puddings among 12 non-stick patty tins (muffin pans) and put in the top of the oven to heat for 2–3 minutes. (Move the potatoes down a shelf.) Stir the batter, pour it into the pans and bake for 15 minutes or until the puddings are risen and golden brown.

6 Meanwhile, steam the broccoli for 10 minutes or until tender, and make the gravy: pour the fat very slowly from the roasting pan, leaving the sediment behind. Place the pan on top of the stove and pour in the stock. Bring to a boil, stirring and scraping up all the browned cooking residue on the bottom of the pan, then simmer until slightly reduced. Season and stir in the remaining mustard, if using.

7 To serve, transfer the meat to a warmed serving platter and surround with the roast potatoes and root vegetables and the Yorkshire puddings. Put the broccoli in a warmed serving dish. Add any meat juices that have collected on the plate to the gravy and stir to combine, then skim off any fat. Pour the gravy into a gravy boat or jug and serve immediately.

Roast beef with a herb crust

A crunchy deep crust of herb-flavoured breadcrumbs ensures a succulent roast beef. It's roasted with a selection of tasty root vegetables and served with a rich gravy, made using the pan juices.

1½ cups (150 g/5 oz) fresh wholemeal (whole-wheat) breadcrumbs
1 tablespoon fennel seeds
6 large sprigs fresh thyme
salt and freshly ground black pepper
¼ cup (60 ml/2 fl oz) olive oil
2 tablespoons milk
1 kg (2 lb) rolled beef topside, trimmed of fat
1 tablespoon wholegrain mustard
1 celeriac (celery root), peeled
2 orange sweet potatoes, peeled
4 carrots, halved lengthwise
300 g (10 oz) French shallots, peeled
100 ml (3½ fl oz) medium–sweet sherry or port

Serves 4
Preparation 25 minutes
Cooking about 2 hours

1 Preheat the oven to 190°C (375°F/Gas 5). Mix the breadcrumbs and fennel seeds in a bowl with the leaves from two of the thyme sprigs and season to taste. Sprinkle 2 tablespoons of the olive oil and the milk over the crumbs and mix thoroughly until they are moist and clump together.

2 Place the beef in a large, lightly oiled roasting pan and spread the meat with the mustard. Press the crumb mixture on the top of the meat, pressing it firmly all over with both hands to make a neat, firm crust. Roast for about 1¾ to 2 hours. Cover the crust loosely with a piece of foil after 1 hour, to prevent overbrowning, then remove the foil for the final 5 minutes of cooking.

3 Meanwhile, cut the celeriac, sweet potatoes and carrots into chunks and place in a large bowl. Add the shallots and the remaining thyme leaves and oil. Mix well. The vegetables require about 1 hour for roasting, so put them in the oven when the beef has been cooking for 45 minutes to 1 hour. Arrange the vegetables around the meat, placing any that won't fit in a separate roasting pan. Turn the vegetables and liberally baste them once during cooking.

4 Remove the meat and vegetables to a warmed serving dish and cover with foil. Pour 300 ml (10 fl oz) water into the roasting pan and bring to the boil on the stove, stirring and scraping up the browned cooking residue. Add the sherry and boil steadily for 5 minutes, stirring from time to time, until the liquid is reduced by about half. Season to taste, then strain the gravy into a jug or gravy boat. Slice the meat and serve with the roast vegetables and gravy.

Herbed roast beef

If you want to serve a great piece of beef, choose a rib roast. It's tasty, supremely tender, a snap to cook, and simple to carve. The 'popover' batter is like Yorkshire pudding batter but is so named because it 'pops' over the top of the muffin tin.

3 kg (6 lb) standing rib roast
1 large clove garlic, halved
1 teaspoon dried t hyme, crumbled
1 teaspoon mustard powder
½ teaspoon dried rosemary, crumbled
½ teaspoon freshly ground black pepper

POPOVERS
½ cup (75 g/2 oz) sifted plain (all-purpose) flour
½ teaspoon salt
½ cup (125 ml/4 fl oz) milk
¼ cup (60 ml/2 fl oz) cold water
2 eggs, lightly beaten
1 tablespoon melted roast beef dripping

Serves 6
Preparation 25 minutes
Cooking about 3 hours

1 For the roast, preheat the oven to 230°C (450°F/Gas 8). Place the roast, fat side up, in a large lightly oiled roasting pan. Rub with garlic. In a small bowl, combine the thyme, mustard, rosemary and pepper, then rub over the roast.

2 Roast, uncovered, for 25 minutes. Reduce the heat to 150°C (300°F/Gas 2) and roast for another 1¾ hours for rare, 2¼ for medium, and 2¾ for well done. Remove the roast from the oven, cover loosely with foil and set aside to rest for 15–20 minutes before carving.

3 For the popovers, increase the oven temperature to 250°C (480°F/Gas 9). Prepare the popovers 30 minutes before the beef is done. Combine the flour and salt in a small bowl. With an electric mixer or rotary beater, beat in the milk a little at a time until smooth. Beat in cold water and the eggs. Cover and set aside in a cool place, but not refrigerated, for about 30 minutes. Beat the batter for about 1½ minutes, until bubbles appear on the surface. Pour ½ teaspoon of the dripping into 6 patty tins (muffin pans) and heat in the oven for 2 minutes, until almost smoking hot. Drop 3 tablespoons of batter into each tin and bake, uncovered, for 8 minutes. Do not open the oven door. Reduce the temperature to 200°C (400°F/Gas 6) and bake for 8 to 10 minutes, until puffy, brown and crisp. Serve at once with the roast beef.

Perfect pot roast

This long-simmered, one-pot meal is wonderfully satisfying. It can be prepared ahead, so it's perfect for family dinners as well as informal entertaining. Serve with a crunchy mixed salad and bread.

1 teaspoon extra virgin olive oil
1 kg (2 lb) piece boneless beef chuck, trimmed of fat and tied
2 large onions, finely chopped
1 stalk celery, finely chopped
3 cloves garlic, crushed
1 cup (250 ml/8 fl oz) dry red or white wine
½ can chopped tomatoes, about 225 g (8 oz)
1 large carrot, grated
1 teaspoon chopped fresh thyme
2 cups (500 ml/16 fl oz) beef stock
500 g (1 lb) new potatoes, quartered
350 g (12 oz) celeriac (celery root), cut into cubes
350 g (12 oz) swede (rutabaga), cut into cubes
4 carrots, about 280 g (10 oz) in total, sliced
salt and freshly ground black pepper
3 tablespoons chopped fresh parsley, to garnish

Serves 6
Preparation 30 minutes
Cooking about 3 hours

1 Preheat the oven to 160°C (320°F/Gas 3). Heat the oil in a large flameproof casserole dish. Add the beef and brown it over a medium–high heat for 6–8 minutes or until it is well coloured on all sides. Remove the meat to a plate.

2 Reduce the heat to medium. Add the onions, celery and garlic and cook, stirring frequently, for about 3 minutes, or until the onions begin to soften. Add the wine and let it bubble for about 1 minute, then add the tomatoes with their juice and the grated carrot. Cook for a further 2 minutes.

3 Return the beef to the dish together with any juices that have collected on the plate and the chopped thyme. Tuck a piece of baking paper or foil around the top of the meat, turning back the corners so that it doesn't touch the liquid, then cover with a tight-fitting lid. Transfer the casserole to the oven and cook for 2½ hours.

4 About 20 minutes before the end of the cooking time, bring the stock to the boil in a deep saucepan with a lid. Add the potatoes, celeriac, swede and sliced carrots. Cover and simmer gently for 12–15 minutes, or until they are starting to become tender.

5 Meanwhile, remove the beef from the dish and set aside. Remove any fat from the cooking liquid, either by spooning it off or by using a bulb baster, then purée the casseroled vegetables and liquid in a blender or food processor until smooth. Season to taste.

6 Drain the potatoes and the other root vegetables, reserving the liquid. Make a layer of the vegetables in the casserole, put the beef on top and add the remaining root vegetables and their cooking liquid. Pour over the puréed sauce. Cover the casserole and return to the oven to cook for 20 minutes or until the root vegetables are tender.

7 Remove the beef to a carving board, cover loosely with foil and leave to rest for 10 minutes. Keep the vegetables and sauce in the oven turned down to low.

8 Carve the beef and arrange on warmed plates with the vegetables and sauce. Sprinkle with the parsley and serve immediately.

Cook's tip

The best cuts of meat for pot roasts are full flavoured, sinewy cuts from the shoulder and hindquarters, including brisket, rump, chuck or round roasts. Long slow cooking tenderises the meat.

Roast beef fillet in red wine

Cancel those dinner reservations – you can make the kind of dinner you find in fine restaurants, and you don't have to be a chef to do it. The fillet almost cooks itself, and the vegetables complement the meat perfectly.

2 kg (4 lb) beef fillet (tenderloin) roast, trimmed
1½ teaspoons coarsely ground black pepper
2 cups (500 ml/16 fl oz) dry red wine
cooking spray
1 kg (2 lb) onions, chopped
3 cloves garlic, crushed
6 sprigs fresh thyme
300 g (10 oz) button mushrooms, trimmed
1 tablespoon sugar
375 g (13 oz) baby carrots
1 punnet (250 g/8 oz) red or yellow cherry tomatoes
500 g (1 lb) wide egg noodles

Serves 10
Preparation 15 minutes
Cooking 2 hours

1 Preheat the oven to 180°C (350°F/Gas 4). Rub the roast with pepper. Tuck the ends under and tie with string. Mix the red wine with 1½ cups (375 ml/13 fl oz) water. Coat a frying pan with cooking spray and set over medium–high heat. Add the beef fillet, a third of the onions and the garlic and sear the meat for 10 minutes, until browned on all sides. Discard the garlic and onion and transfer the fillet to a roasting pan. Pour in half the wine mixture. Add 3 thyme sprigs and place the pan in the oven.

2 Meanwhile, set aside 5 mushrooms and slice the remaining ones. Sauté the mushrooms, remaining onions and sugar in the frying pan for about 7 minutes, until brown. Cook the carrots in a saucepan of boiling water for 5–7 minutes, until they are just tender. Drain.

3 After the meat has been roasting for 20 minutes, add the carrots and sautéed vegetables to the pan. Pour in the remaining wine mixture. Roast the beef for a further 1¼ hours for rare, 1¾ hours for medium and 2 hours for well done. Transfer the meat to a carving board, cover loosely with foil and leave to rest for 10 minutes. Add the tomatoes to the pan, cover and set aside.

4 Meanwhile, cook the noodles according to the packet directions. Trim the reserved mushrooms and flute with a paring knife. Coat a frying pan with cooking spray and set over medium heat. Sauté the mushrooms for 5 minutes. Arrange the noodles and vegetables on a platter. Slice the beef and add to the platter. Garnish with mushrooms and thyme and serve with the pan juices.

Lamb with herb and garlic rub

Lamb is best teamed with herbs that pack a punch, as this trio of thyme, rosemary and parsley does. Also try a combination of oregano, thyme and mint or coriander. The flavours of the herb rub will permeate the meat.

2 kg (4 lb) leg of lamb
1 lemon, halved and seeded

HERB AND GARLIC RUB
3 tablespoons finely chopped fresh thyme
2 tablespoons finely chopped fresh rosemary
2 tablespoons finely chopped fresh parsley
8 cloves garlic, finely chopped
1 tablespoon sea salt flakes
½ teaspoon freshly ground black pepper
¼ cup (60 ml/2 fl oz) olive oil

Serves 6
Preparation 20 minutes + 1 hour marinating
Cooking 2 hours

1 To make the rub, mix the herbs, garlic, salt and pepper in a medium bowl. Pour in the oil and mix until well combined.

2 Using a sharp knife, make several small slits all over lamb. Rub the herb mixture all over the meat, pushing it into the slits, then leave the lamb for 1 hour at room temperature to marinate.

3 Preheat the oven to 180°C (350°F/Gas 4). Place the lamb in a roasting pan, fat side up, and cook for about 2 hours (30 minutes per 500 g/1 lb). Cover with foil after 1 hour.

4 Transfer the lamb to a carving board. Squeeze the lemon juice over lamb, then allow to rest for about 10–15 minutes before slicing. Serve with roasted vegetables and steamed beans.

Cook's tip

It is important to rest a joint of meat for at least 10 minutes before carving and serving. When rested, the internal and external temperatures even out and the juices are redistributed, making the meat more succulent and easier to carve.

Mediterranean roasted lamb

Just a few fresh ingredients, simply cooked, make a warmly satisfying meal. Eggplants and shallots, whose flavours intensify with roasting, make perfect partners for tender, succulent lamb. Serve with warm, crusty bread.

¼ cup (60 ml/2 fl oz) olive oil
1 teaspoon balsamic or red wine vinegar
4 lean lamb leg steaks, trimmed of fat
2 teaspoons black peppercorns
1 teaspoon cumin seeds
250 g (9 oz) French shallots, unpeeled
2 large eggplants (aubergine)
2 cloves garlic, crushed
400 g (14 oz) cherry tomatoes, pricked
salt and freshly ground black pepper
1 tablespoon chopped fresh coriander (cilantro)

Serves 4
Preparation 20 minutes
+ several hours marinating
Cooking 45 minutes

1 Mix 1 tablespoon of the oil with the vinegar and lightly brush this marinade over both sides of the steaks. Crush the peppercorns and add the cumin seeds. Sprinkle the mixture over the steaks, pat it in gently and then place the steaks in a non-metallic dish. Set aside, or cover and refrigerate for several hours.

2 Preheat the oven to 200°C (400°F/Gas 6). Put the shallots in a large, heatproof bowl and pour over enough boiling water to cover. Leave for 2–3 minutes, then drain. Peel off the skins, then return them to the bowl.

3 Trim the ends from the eggplants, cut them into chunks and add to the shallots. Drizzle the remaining oil over the vegetables. Add the crushed garlic, then toss to lightly coat the vegetables with oil.

4 Heat a large, heavy-based roasting pan on the stove over a medium–high heat. Sear the steaks for about 1 minute on each side, then remove and set aside in the original marinade dish.

5 Tip the vegetables into the hot pan and spread them out. Place in the oven and roast for 15–20 minutes until softened. Lay the lamb steaks over the vegetables and drizzle any juices left in the dish over the lamb. Return to the oven to roast for 10 minutes. Scatter the tomatoes into the pan and return to the oven for a further 8–10 minutes, until the lamb is cooked to your liking and the vegetables are tender. Season to taste and serve sprinkled with coriander.

Roast leg of lamb with beans

Lamb and flageolet beans are often served together in French country cooking because they complement each other so well. In this recipe the flageolets are mixed with potatoes and green beans.

250 g (9 oz) dried flageolet or cannellini beans
4 large cloves garlic, peeled
1 bay leaf
1 kg (2 lb) boneless leg of lamb, trimmed of fat
salt and freshly ground black pepper
4 small sprigs fresh rosemary
½ lemon, thinly sliced
2 teaspoons olive oil
500 g (1 lb) potatoes, peeled
4 tomatoes, diced
4 tablespoons chopped fresh parsley
500 g (1 lb) green beans
4 tablespoons red wine
300 ml (10 fl oz) lamb or beef stock

Serves 6
Preparation 20 minutes + overnight soaking
Cooking about 1½ hours

1 Soak the flageolets overnight in water. Drain and rinse, then place them in a large saucepan and pour over enough cold water to come up to about twice the depth of the beans. Cover the pan with its lid and bring to a boil. Skim off any scum, then reduce the heat and add 2 of the garlic cloves and the bay leaf. Cover the pan again and cook the beans over low heat for about 1¼ hours or until tender.

2 Meanwhile, preheat the oven to 180°C (350°F/Gas 4). Untie the lamb if necessary, season the inside with salt and pepper and sprinkle over the leaves from half of the rosemary sprigs. Place the lemon slices down the middle, then roll up the meat and tie it with string at 2.5 cm (1 inch) intervals. Rub the outside of the joint with 1 teaspoon of the oil and season to taste. Cut the remaining garlic cloves into slivers. With the tip of a knife, cut slits in the lamb and insert the garlic slivers and the remaining rosemary, broken into little sprigs.

3 Set the lamb rounded side up, on a rack in a shallow roasting pan. Transfer to the oven and roast for 1 hour for rare, 1¼ hours for medium and 1½ hours for well done.

4 About 30 minutes before the lamb is ready, cut the potatoes into cubes and cook in boiling water for about 10 minutes, or until just tender, then drain well. When the lamb is done, transfer it to a carving board, cover loosely with foil to keep warm and set aside to rest. Drain off any fat from the roasting pan.

5 Heat the remaining 1 teaspoon oil in a large saucepan over medium heat. Add the tomatoes and cook for 3–4 minutes. Drain the cooked beans and discard the bay leaf. Add the beans to the tomato, then add the parsley. Cover and cook for a further 3 minutes, then gently stir in the potatoes. Season to taste and keep warm over low heat.

6 Put the green beans in a saucepan and barely cover with boiling water. Cook over medium heat for 3–4 minutes, or until just tender. Drain well and keep warm.

7 To make the gravy, place the roasting pan on top of the stove and pour in the wine and stock. Bring to the boil over medium heat, stirring and scraping the bottom of the pan to mix in any cooking residue, then boil for 1 minute. Keep hot over low heat.

8 Carve the lamb. Put the bean and potato mixture on a warmed serving platter and arrange the slices of lamb on top. Serve the gravy and green beans separately.

Cook's tip

To save time, use canned beans, drained and rinsed.

Roast leg of lamb with rosemary

A succulent roast leg of lamb never goes out of fashion and the garlic and rosemary complement the lamb perfectly. Roast some potatoes, pumpkin and carrots at the same time for an easy, delicious meal.

6 sprigs fresh rosemary
2 kg (4 lb) bone-in leg of lamb
2 cloves garlic, sliced
2 tablespoons olive oil
salt and freshly ground black pepper
1 bulb garlic, halved

Serves 8
Preparation 15 minutes
Cooking 1½ hours

1 Preheat the oven to 220°C (425°F/Gas 7).

2 Cut 2 sprigs of rosemary into short lengths. Using a sharp knife make holes evenly over the lamb and push the cut rosemary and sliced garlic into the slits. Rub all over with the olive oil and season with salt and freshly ground black pepper.

3 Place the remaining rosemary sprigs in a roasting pan with the garlic bulb and lamb. Roast for 20 minutes then reduce the heat to 180°C (350°F/Gas 4) and cook for 1 to 1½ hours or until cooked to your liking.

4 One hour before the lamb is ready, add the vegetables of your choice to the roasting pan or roast in a separate pan. Rest the meat for 15 minutes before carving.

Cook's tip

Cut the vegetables of your choice into even-sized chunks and put them in the oven to cook about 1 hour before the roast lamb has finished cooking. Place them around the leg of lamb or in a separate roasting pan.

Herb-crusted leg of lamb

The distinctive flavour of lamb responds well to certain seasonings. Garlic, oregano, rosemary, mint, thyme and lemon are the most traditional. The seasonings can be patted on the leg before roasting or inserted into the flesh.

2 tablespoons chopped fresh parsley
1 tablespoon chopped fresh rosemary or
  1 teaspoon dried rosemary, crumbled
1 tablespoon chopped fresh thyme or
  1 teaspoon dried thyme, crumbled
1 tablespoon chopped fresh mint or
  1 teaspoon mint flakes
1 tablespoon olive oil
1 tablespoon balsamic vinegar
1 tablespoon dijon mustard
1 teaspoon salt
½ teaspoon freshly ground black pepper
1 whole leg of lamb (about 3 kg/6 lb)
2 cloves garlic, cut into thin slivers

Serves 8
Preparation 15 minutes
Cooking about 1½ hours

1 Preheat the oven to 230°C (450°F/Gas 8). In a small bowl, combine all the ingredients except the lamb and garlic.

2 Place the lamb, fat side up, on a rack in a shallow roasting pan. With a small sharp knife, cut twelve slits, each 1 cm long and 1 cm deep, about 5 cm apart (½ inch slits, about 2 inches apart), in the top of the lamb. Insert slivers of garlic into each slit, pushing them into the meat.

3 Spread the herb mixture evenly over the lamb. Roast, uncovered, for 15 minutes. Reduce the oven temperature to 180°C (350°F/Gas 4) and roast, uncovered, for another 1¼ hours.

4 Remove from the oven and transfer to a carving board, cover loosely with foil and allow to rest for 15–20 minutes before carving.

Roast shoulder of lamb

A boned shoulder of lamb makes an easy-to-carve roast. The fruit stuffing in this recipe complements the lamb perfectly. For a complete meal, serve with roast potatoes and carrots and steamed green beans.

STUFFING
1 cup (80 g/2½ oz) fresh breadcrumbs
½ cup (100 g/3½ oz) chopped dried apricots
¼ cup (35 g/1 oz) currants
¼ cup (15 g/½ oz) chopped fresh parsley
2 tablespoons butter, melted

1.5 kg (3 lb) shoulder of lamb, boned
olive oil, for brushing
¼ cup (60 g/2 oz) mint jelly, warmed
2 cups (500 ml/16 fl oz) beef stock

Serves 6
Preparation 15 minutes
Cooking 1½ hours

1 Preheat the oven to 180°C (350°C/Gas 4). Put all the stuffing ingredients in a bowl and mix together well.

2 Press the fruit stuffing onto the cut side of the lamb. Roll the lamb up to secure the stuffing, then tie the lamb at regular intervals with kitchen string to hold its shape. Rub the lamb with some olive oil and season well with salt and freshly ground black pepper.

3 Place the lamb in a roasting pan and roast for 50 minutes. Mix the mint jelly with ¼ cup (60 ml/2 fl oz) hot water, then pour over the lamb. Reduce the oven temperature to 160°C (320°F/Gas 2–3). Cover the roasting dish with foil and roast the lamb for a further 40 minutes.

4 Remove the lamb from the roasting pan to a carving board, loosely cover with foil and allow to rest for 15–20 minutes before carving.

5 While the lamb is resting, make the gravy. Place the roasting pan on the stovetop and pour in the stock, stirring well to scrape up any stuck-on residue. Bring to a boil, then reduce the heat and simmer for 5 minutes, or until the liquid has reduced. Strain into a gravy boat or jug.

6 Slice the lamb and serve with pan gravy, roast potatoes and carrots and steamed beans.

Stuffed roast pork with prunes

Pork and prunes is a classic French combination, and here it is given an extra boost with ginger and orange. Cooked with a variety of vegetables it makes an easy roast meal. Prepare ahead and keep in the refrigerator ready for cooking.

2 small pork fillets (tenderloins) (about 175 g/6 oz each)
1 large orange
⅓ cup (50 g/1¾ oz) sliced prunes
3 knobs stem ginger in syrup, drained and thinly sliced
salt and freshly ground black pepper
6 slices rindless bacon
500 g (1 lb) new potatoes, cut into slices
2 leeks, trimmed and thickly sliced
2 carrots, thickly sliced
2 red apples
2 cups (500 ml/16 fl oz) dry alcoholic cider
2 tablespoons chopped fresh flat-leaf parsley

Serves 4
Preparation 25 minutes
Cooking about 1 hour

1 Preheat the oven to 200°C (400°F/Gas 6). Cut each pork fillet in half lengthwise, without cutting all the way through. Open the fillets like a book and press down to flatten slightly.

2 Finely grate the zest from the orange and set aside. Using a small, serrated knife, cut away all the white pith from the orange, then slice down between the membranes to remove the orange segments. Arrange the orange segments over the cut surface of one fillet. Top with the sliced prunes and ginger, sprinkle with the orange zest, then season to taste.

3 Place the second fillet, cut-side down, on top and gently press the fillets together. Wrap the bacon slices around the pork and secure in place with kitchen string. Set aside.

4 Spread the potatoes over the base of a large roasting pan, then scatter over the leeks and carrots. Core and thickly slice the apples, then add to the pan. Place the pork-fillet package on top and pour in the cider. Roast for 1 hour, or until the potatoes and carrots are tender and clear juices come out of the pork when it is pierced with the tip of a knife. Lift out the pork and vegetables, cover with foil to keep warm and leave to rest for 10 minutes.

5 Meanwhile, put the roasting pan on the stove and boil the cooking liquid over high heat until it is reduced to about ⅔ cup (170 ml/5½ fl oz). Add the parsley and season to taste. Slice the pork and serve with the vegetables and the cooking juices spooned over the top.

Gingered roast pork

Roast pork with apple sauce, an all-time favourite, is given a new twist in this dish inspired by German cuisine. It is absolutely delicious served with roast potatoes and seasonal green vegetables.

1 kg (2 lb) boned pork loin without skin, trimmed of fat
3 sweet apples
1 small onion, finely chopped
75 g (2½ oz) ready-to-eat prunes, chopped
75 g (2½ oz) gingersnap biscuits, crushed
1 egg yolk
salt and freshly ground black pepper
300 ml (10 fl oz) chicken stock
200 ml (7 fl oz) dry white wine
4 tablespoons extra virgin olive oil
1 kg (2 lb) parsnips, quartered
1 tablespoon honey
500 g (1 lb) French shallots

Serves 6
Preparation 30 minutes
Cooking 2 hours

1 Preheat oven to 180°C (350°F/Gas 4). Place the pork, skinned side down, on a chopping board. Slit the joint lengthwise, cutting two-thirds of the way through the meat, then open it out like a book.

2 Peel, core and finely chop 1 of the apples, then mix with the onion, prunes, biscuits, egg yolk and seasoning to taste. Spoon onto the pork, spreading evenly, then press the joint back together. Tie into a neat shape with string.

3 Put the joint, skinned side up, into a roasting pan and pour in the stock and wine. Cover the pan with foil, twisting the ends tightly over the edges. Transfer to the oven and roast for 2 hours.

4 After 45 minutes, heat the oil in a second roasting pan on the shelf above the pork for 5 minutes. Add the parsnips and leave to roast, turning them once or twice.

5 Meanwhile, make the Apple sauce with ginger (see page 142).

6 When the pork has been cooking for 1¼ hours, remove the foil and drizzle the meat with the honey. Add the shallots to the parsnips, toss together and continue roasting.

7 About 20 minutes before the end of the cooking time, peel, core and thickly slice the remaining 2 apples, then add them to the vegetables.

8 Transfer the pork to a carving board, cover loosely with foil to keep warm and leave to rest. Strain the cooking liquid into a saucepan, then skim off any fat. Boil the cooking liquid, stirring constantly, for 2 minutes. Pour into a gravy boat or jug.

9 Carve the pork and serve immediately, with the roasted vegetables, apple sauce and gravy.

Cook's tip

As a change from roast vegetables, serve with puréed celeriac (celery root). Cook 1 kg (2 lb) diced celeriac in boiling water for 15 minutes, then mash or purée with 4 tablespoons milk. Season to taste.

Pork with apples, celery and walnuts

Fresh and fruity, this dish comes from Normandy in northwestern France, where cider apples grow in profusion. A dish of rice is cooked in the oven at the same time, making this a very simple meal to prepare.

2 tablespoons sunflower oil
500 g (1 lb) pork fillets (tenderloins), trimmed of fat and cut into cubes
8 stalks celery, cut across into 5 cm (2 inch) lengths, leaves reserved and chopped
1 onion, roughly chopped
2 cups (500 ml/16 fl oz) cider or apple juice
1 bay leaf
salt and freshly ground black pepper
1½ cups (300 g/10 oz) long-grain white rice
4 cups (1 litre/35 fl oz) hot chicken stock
3 crisp sweet apples, preferably red-skinned
¾ cup (100 g/3½ oz) broken walnuts

Serves 4
Preparation 15 minutes
Cooking about 1½ hours

1 Preheat the oven to 160°C (320°F/Gas 2–3). Heat the oil in a deep roasting pan, add the pork and fry, stirring frequently, for 5 minutes, or until browned on all sides. Add the celery and onion and fry gently for about 10 minutes, or until softened.

2 Pour in the cider or apple juice and add the bay leaf. Season to taste. Bring to a boil, then cover with foil and transfer to the oven. Cook for 1¼ hours, or until the pork is tender.

3 About 40 minutes before the pork is ready, put the rice in a small baking dish and pour over the hot stock. Stir well, then cover and place in the oven to cook with the pork.

4 About 25 minutes before the end of the cooking time, quarter and core the apples but do not peel them. Slice the quarters thickly, then add to the pork and continue cooking.

5 Meanwhile, heat a small frying pan over medium heat, add the walnuts and cook, stirring, until lightly toasted. When the pork is tender, stir in the walnuts and taste for seasoning. Garnish with the chopped celery leaves and serve hot, with the rice. Serve with vegetables such as steamed green beans or snow peas.

Mustard-roast ham with parsnips

This is an excellent way of cooking all your vegetables with a joint of meat in one pan. Parsnips as well as zucchini and red onions provide a colourful and delicious mixture that goes beautifully with ham.

1 boneless, unsmoked ham (about 1.5 kg/3 lb), with its skin on (soaked if necessary)
1 bay leaf
12 large parsnips, quartered lengthwise
2 red onions, each cut into six wedges
¼ cup (60 ml/2 fl oz) vegetable oil
20 cloves
1 tablespoon dijon mustard
1 tablespoon honey
1 tablespoon soft brown sugar
3 zucchini (courgettes), thickly sliced
1 tablespoon sesame seeds
freshly ground black pepper

Serves 8
Preparation 25 minutes
Cooking about 2 hours

1 Put the ham in a large saucepan with the bay leaf and enough cold water to cover it. Slowly bring to a boil, skimming off any froth that rises to the surface. Reduce the heat, cover and gently simmer for 40 minutes. Remove the ham and set aside but keep the water at a simmer.

2 Preheat the oven to 180°C (350°F/Gas 4) and put a large roasting pan in to heat. Add the parsnips and onions to the simmering water, bring back to a boil and cook for 2 minutes, then drain. Leave to cool for a few minutes, then return to the pan. Drizzle with 2½ tablespoons of the oil and toss to coat. Tip the vegetables into the roasting pan and roast for 20 minutes.

3 Meanwhile, use a sharp knife to cut the rind off the ham, leaving a thin, even layer of fat. Score deep lines across the fat, cutting into the flesh slightly so the glaze can penetrate, then score the fat in the opposite direction to make neat diamond shapes. Stud the ham with cloves. Blend the mustard, honey and sugar together, then spread over the fat. Push the vegetables to the sides of the pan, put the ham in the middle, roast for 10 minutes. Increase the temperature to 220°C (425°F/Gas 7). Toss the zucchini in the remaining oil. Add to the pan, turning the vegetables at the same time, then roast for a further 30 minutes until the ham is well glazed and golden. To check the ham is cooked, insert a skewer into the centre — when removed the juices should run clear.

4 Remove the ham, cover with foil. Turn the vegetables, then sprinkle with sesame seeds and black pepper. Roast for a final 5 minutes. Slice the ham and serve hot, with the vegetables.

Baked ham with brown sugar glaze

Using a bone-in ham for this recipe is important because the bone intensifies the flavour of the meat. Each serving should include a bit of crust; its sweetness complements the saltiness of the meat.

4 kg (8 lb) fully cooked, bone-in shank portion smoked ham
½ cup (115 g/4 oz) firmly packed brown sugar
2 tablespoons bourbon or orange juice
1¼ teaspoons freshly ground black pepper or 1½ teaspoons grated orange zest

Serves 16
Preparation 15 minutes
Cooking about 2½ hours

1 Preheat the oven to 170°C (340°F/Gas 3). Remove the skin, if any, from the ham and trim the fat to a thickness of 5 mm (¼ inch).

2 Place the ham, cut side down, on a wire rack in a shallow roasting pan. Bake the ham, uncovered, for about 2 to 2¾ hours. If the ham browns too fast, cover loosely with foil. Meanwhile, combine the sugar, bourbon (or orange juice) and pepper (or orange zest) in a small bowl.

3 Remove the ham from the oven and increase the temperature to 190°C (375°F/Gas 5). Using a sharp paring knife, score the fat on the surface of the ham in a diamond pattern. Brush the sugar mixture over the ham.

4 Return the ham to the oven and bake for about 15–20 minutes. Remove to a carving board, cover loosely with foil and allow to rest for at least 15 minutes before carving.

Baked ham with pineapple glaze

Long before turkey became a Christmas dinner institution, there was baked ham. The ham can be prepared for glazing the day before, then covered and refrigerated before cooking. Baked ham is also delicious served cold.

7 kg (15 lb) ham, cooked on the bone
cloves, to decorate
1 cup (350 g/12 oz) honey
¼ cup (60 ml/2 fl oz) pineapple juice
1 cup (185 g/6½ oz) lightly packed brown sugar
2 teaspoons dijon mustard

Serves 20–25
Preparation about 1 hour
Cooking ¾–1¾ hours

1 To prepare the pre-cooked ham, strip off the brown skin, trying not to disturb the layer of creamy fat beneath it. Score the surface of the fat into small diamonds and stud each diamond with a clove. Line a large roasting pan with a double thickness of foil, bringing the foil over the edges of the pan. (This will catch drips of glaze falling off the ham and prevent flare-ups. It also means a clean roasting pan at the end of cooking time.) Put the ham in the pan, making sure the foil stays upright.

2 Preheat the oven to 220°C (425°F/Gas 7). Mix the glaze ingredients together, pour over the ham and put it in the oven. If you are glazing for appearance only, it will take about 45 minutes.

3 As parts of the fat take on enough colour, a rich golden brown with slightly charred edges, place small pieces of foil on top to deflect the heat. If you want to serve the ham hot, allow an hour longer for it to heat through (about 1½–1¾ hours in total), but lower the heat to 200°C (400°F/Gas 6) after 1 hour. (You may need to protect the entire surface of the ham with foil after 50–60 minutes. The ham should be basted with the glaze every 20 minutes or so.)

4 Serve the ham hot or at room temperature. Use a long, thin-bladed knife to slice it. Cut the first slice vertically, down to the bone, in the centre of the leg, then slice at a slight angle on either side of this cut. This gives every slice of ham (until you get closer to the bone) a rim of glaze-encrusted fat. To refrigerate the ham, wrap in clean muslin (cheesecloth); it keeps up to a week.

Poultry

Roast herb and garlic chicken

Rather than rubbing oil or butter over a bird before roasting, here a paste of fresh herbs and ricotta cheese is pushed under the skin. This keeps the chicken beautifully moist during roasting and imparts a wonderful flavour.

1 lemon
1 chicken, about 1.5 kg (3 lb), without giblets
½ cup (15 g/½ oz) fresh coriander (cilantro)
½ cup (15 g/½ oz) fresh parsley
2 cloves garlic, peeled
2 tablespoons ricotta or fromage frais
salt and freshly ground black pepper
150 ml (5 fl oz) dry white wine
lemon slices, to garnish
sprigs of fresh coriander or parsley, to garnish

Serves 4
Preparation 15 minutes
Cooking 1¾ – 2 hours

1 Preheat the oven to 180°C (350°F/Gas 4). Grate and reserve the zest from the lemon, then cut the lemon in half. Rinse the chicken inside and out, then pat dry with paper towels. Hold the chicken on its end in a small roasting pan and squeeze the lemon juice inside the cavity (make sure the juice doesn't run out the other end). Push the lemon halves inside the cavity and sprinkle in half the zest.

2 Place the chicken in the pan, breast side up. Very carefully ease your fingers under the skin, starting at the neck end. Loosen the skin over the breasts and thighs, without breaking it. Combine the herbs and garlic in a food processor or small blender and process until finely chopped. Add the ricotta and remaining lemon zest. Season with salt and black pepper and briefly process again to mix. (Alternatively, finely chop the herbs and garlic with a knife, then mix with the other ingredients.) Push the paste under the skin, easing it along so that it covers the breasts and thighs evenly in a thin layer. Secure the end of the neck skin by folding the wing tips under.

3 Cover the chicken with foil and roast for 45 minutes. Remove the foil and roast, uncovered, for a further 1–1¼ hours, or until the juices run clear when a skewer is inserted into the thickest part of the thigh. Baste once or twice with the pan juices. Lift up the chicken, tipping it so the juices run out of the cavity into the pan. Remove the chicken to a carving board, cover loosely with foil to keep warm, and set aside to rest.

4 Skim the fat from the roasting pan juices, then place the pan on the stovetop and bring the juices to a boil. Add the wine and bring back to a boil, scraping up the browned bits. Boil for 1 minute and season to taste. Carve the chicken. Garnish with lemon and herb sprigs and serve with the gravy.

Best-ever roast chicken with gravy

You really won't find an easier recipe for roast chicken, but it's utterly delicious. Do use the best-quality bird you can afford because its superior flavour will really shine through.

1 chicken, about 2.5 kg (5 lb), without giblets
salt and freshly ground black pepper
butter, for greasing

GRAVY
2 cups (500 ml/16 fl oz) chicken or vegetable stock, or water
3 tablespoons plain (all-purpose) flour

Serves 6
Preparation 10 minutes
Cooking 2 hours

1 Preheat the oven to 200°C (400°F/Gas 6). Rinse the chicken, then pat dry with paper towels. Season the chicken inside and out with salt and black pepper, tie the legs together with kitchen string, then brush with butter.

2 Place the chicken, breast side up, on a wire rack in a roasting pan. Roast, uncovered, for 30 minutes.

3 Reduce the oven temperature to 180°C (350°F/Gas 4) and continue to roast the chicken, basting every 20 minutes with the pan juices, for about 1¼ hours, until the juices run clear when a skewer is inserted into the thickest part of the thigh. Remove the chicken to a carving board, cover loosely with foil to keep warm, and set aside to rest while you make the pan gravy.

4 For the gravy, skim the fat from the roasting pan juices. Place the pan over medium heat, pour in ½ cup (125 ml/4 fl oz) of the stock and simmer for 1 minute, scraping up all the browned bits from the bottom of the pan. Transfer to a saucepan. Blend the flour with ¼ cup (60 ml/2 fl oz) of the remaining stock and add to the saucepan. Set over medium heat and whisk constantly until blended. Gradually add the stock and cook, stirring, for about 3 minutes, until the mixture boils and thickens slightly. Season to taste.

5 Carve the chicken into slices or serving pieces and serve with the gravy.

Ginger and hoisin chicken wings

For a roast dinner with a difference, these chicken wings are delectable. They are deliciously sticky, so keep some paper napkins handy for messy fingers (or just lick your fingers when no-one's looking)!

1.5 kg (3 lb 5 oz) chicken wings
⅓ cup (80 ml/2½ fl oz) hoisin sauce
¼ cup (90 g/3¼ oz) maple syrup or honey
3 cloves garlic, chopped
2 cm (¾ inch) piece fresh ginger, peeled and finely chopped
2 teaspoons sesame oil

Serves 4
Preparation 10 minutes + marinating
Cooking 45–50 minutes

1 Rinse the chicken wings, then pat dry with paper towels. Using a sharp knife, cut through the joints of the wings so you end up with three pieces. Discard the small wing 'tip'. Place the other pieces on a large baking tray lined with baking paper.

2 To prepare the marinade, mix the hoisin sauce, maple syrup or honey, garlic, ginger and sesame oil in a small bowl until combined. Pour the marinade over the chicken and, using clean hands, gently mix until the chicken is coated. Cover with plastic wrap and marinate in the refrigerator for at least 4 hours, or preferably overnight, to allow the flavours to soak in. Toss the chicken wings in the marinade occasionally to ensure they stay well coated.

3 Preheat the oven to 200°C (400°F/Gas 6). Bake the chicken wings for 45–50 minutes, turning them after 20–25 minutes. Toss regularly during the last 15 minutes of cooking, as the sauce will caramelise and form a glaze over the chicken.

Cook's tip

To make this a main meal, serve with rice and steamed vegetables. Drizzle with any cooking juices from the chicken before serving.

Roast chicken with herb stuffing

When it comes to a Sunday lunch or a special dinner, it's hard to beat roast chicken – especially one that comes replete with gravy and a fragrant fresh herb stuffing! Try a mixture of thyme, sage, parsley and tarragon.

1 chicken, about 2 kg (4 lb), without giblets
1 lemon, quartered
butter, for greasing
2 teaspoons olive oil
lemon wedges, to serve

Serves 6
Preparation 30 minutes
Cooking 2¼ hours

STUFFING
25 g (1 oz) butter
1 tablespoon olive oil
1 onion, finely chopped
2 celery stalks, finely chopped
1¼ cups (125 g/4 oz) fresh white breadcrumbs
1½ tablespoons chopped fresh mixed herbs
1 egg, beaten
salt and freshly ground black pepper

1 Preheat the oven to 220°C (425°F/Gas 7). To make the stuffing, gently heat the butter and oil in a large frying pan over medium heat and sauté the onion and celery for 10 minutes, or until soft. Tip into a bowl, stir in the breadcrumbs, herbs and egg. Season with salt and pepper and mix well to bind the mixture together. Allow to cool completely.

2 Rinse the chicken inside and out, then pat dry with paper towels. Loosely stuff the chicken with half the stuffing, pushing it well up inside the cavity to make a neat shape. Put the lemon quarters in the cavity and tie the legs together with kitchen string. Put the remaining stuffing in a lightly buttered ovenproof dish.

3 Place the chicken, breast side down, on a wire rack in a roasting pan. Pour in about 1 cup (250 ml/9 fl oz) water (the steam this creates will keep the bird moist). Roast for 30 minutes.

4 Remove the pan from the oven and carefully turn the chicken breast side up. Rub the olive oil over the breast, then season with salt and pepper. Reduce the oven temperature to 150°C (300°F/Gas 2) and roast for a further 1 hour, basting every 20 minutes with the pan juices. Put the dish of stuffing in the oven and roast the chicken, basting as before, for a final 30 minutes, or until the juices run clear when a skewer is inserted into the thickest part of the thigh.

5 Tip the bird up slightly so any lemony juices inside the cavity run into the pan. Remove the chicken to a carving board, cover loosely with foil to keep warm, and set aside to rest while making the gravy. Keep the stuffing in a warm place. Meanwhile, make the gravy.

6 Carve the chicken and serve with the stuffing, gravy and some lemon wedges.

Cook's tip

To make the gravy, mix 1½ tablespoons plain (all-purpose) flour with 3 tablespoons water to form a paste. Gradually stir in the pan juices from the chicken until smooth, then pour the mixture into a saucepan. Add 150 ml (5 fl oz) chicken stock, 150 ml (5 fl oz) water and 150 ml (5 fl oz) wine or apple juice, then bring to a boil over medium heat, stirring until smooth and thickened. Season to taste.

Middle Eastern roast chicken

This chicken is roasted with a fig and pistachio couscous stuffing and basted with a spicy lemon marinade to keep the flesh deliciously moist. A leafy salad with fresh oranges would make a great side dish.

1 chicken, about 1.5 kg (3 lb), without giblets
butter, for greasing
grated zest and juice of 1 lemon
1 tablespoon honey
2 tablespoons olive oil
½ teaspoon ground ginger
½ teaspoon ground cinnamon
1 teaspoon ground cumin
freshly ground black pepper
3 small red onions, each cut into six wedges

COUSCOUS STUFFING
1⅔ cups (300 g/10 oz) couscous
¼ teaspoon saffron threads
2 cups (500 ml/16 fl oz) chicken stock, hot
⅓ cup (75 g/2½ oz) chopped dried figs
⅓ cup (50 g/2 oz) shelled unsalted pistachios, roughly chopped

Serves 4–6
Preparation 30 minutes
Cooking 1½ hours

1 Rinse the chicken inside and out, then pat dry with paper towels. Place in a large, lightly buttered roasting pan. Mix the lemon zest and juice with the honey, olive oil, ginger, cinnamon, cumin and black pepper to taste. Brush some of the marinade generously inside the cavity of the bird, then over the outside, reserving the rest of the marinade. Leave the flavours to infuse while making the stuffing (or for longer, if convenient).

2 Preheat the oven to 180°C (350°F/Gas 4). Put the couscous in a heatproof bowl. Stir the saffron into the stock, then pour it over the couscous. Cover and leave to stand for 5 minutes, or until all the stock has been absorbed. Stir in the figs and pistachios and season to taste with salt and pepper. Spoon some of the couscous stuffing into the neck end of the chicken. Fold the neck skin over and tie the legs together with kitchen string. Arrange the onion wedges in the pan around the bird after it has been roasting for 40 minutes. Spoon the reserved marinade over the chicken and roast for 1 hour.

3 Spoon the remaining couscous mixture around the chicken and roast for a further 25 minutes, or until the juices run clear when a skewer is inserted into the thickest part of the thigh. Remove the chicken to a carving board, cover loosely with foil to keep warm, and set aside to rest for 10 minutes before carving. Carve the chicken and serve with the couscous and onions.

Golden-roasted chicken with stuffing

Here's a great one for when you're feeling nostalgic. The herb bread stuffing is an old-fashioned favourite. It's just as welcome on a fancy dinner table as it is for a simple family dinner.

2 tablespoons fresh thyme leaves, plus a few sprigs
2 tablespoons chopped fresh sage
freshly ground black pepper
1 chicken, about 1.5 kg (3 lb), without giblets
1 lemon, thinly sliced
1 tablespoon olive oil
3 onions, chopped
3 stalks celery, chopped
2 cups (500 ml/16 fl oz) chicken stock
4 cups (400 g/14 oz) dry breadcrumbs

Serves 6
Preparation 30 minutes
Cooking 2¼ hours

1 Preheat the oven to 220°C (425°F/Gas 7). Mix the thyme, sage and some black pepper to taste in a small bowl. Rinse the chicken inside and out, then pat dry with paper towels. Gently separate the chicken skin from the breast and insert a third of the herb mixture and lemon slices under the skin. Sprinkle another third of the herb mixture inside and over the chicken.

2 Heat the olive oil in a large frying pan over medium–high heat. Sauté the onions and celery for about 5 minutes, until soft. Stir in the remaining herb mixture. Pour in half the stock and 1 cup (250 ml/8 fl oz) water and bring to a boil. Add the breadcrumbs and toss until the liquid has been completely absorbed. Remove from the heat.

3 Loosely stuff the stuffing mixture into the neck end of the chicken, then insert a few thyme sprigs into the cavity. Tie the legs together with kitchen string. Place the chicken, breast side down, on a wire rack in a roasting pan. Pour in the remaining stock and 1 cup (250 ml/8 fl oz) water. Roast for 30 minutes, then remove the pan from the oven and carefully turn the chicken breast side up. Reduce the oven temperature to 180°C (350°F/Gas 4) and roast, basting every 20 minutes with the pan juices, for 1½ hours, or until the juices run clear when a skewer is inserted into the thickest part of the thigh.

4 Remove the chicken to a carving board. Transfer the stuffing to a bowl, discarding the thyme sprigs, and keep in a warm place. Cover the chicken loosely with foil to keep warm, and set aside to rest for 10 minutes before carving. Carve, discard the lemon slices and serve with the stuffing.

Roast turkey with lemon couscous

A small turkey like this is amazingly economical. It will give enough meat for at least 8 portions, or you can serve 4 people and have plenty of leftovers for sandwiches, salads and other dishes.

4 large lemons
1¾ cups (325 g/11½ oz) couscous
1 teaspoon ground turmeric
1 teaspoon ground cumin
1 teaspoon ground cinnamon
4 cups (1 litre/35 fl oz) chicken or turkey stock, hot
⅔ cup (115 g/4 oz) chopped dried apricots
4 tablespoons chopped fresh mint, plus mint sprigs, to garnish
1 turkey, about 2.5 kg (5 lb), without giblets
150 ml (5 fl oz) dry sherry
salt and freshly ground black pepper

Serves 8
Preparation 20 minutes + 10 minutes soaking
Cooking 2 hours

1 Halve the lemons lengthwise and squeeze all the juice into a bowl. Pull the membranes and pulp from each lemon half to leave a smooth clean shell. Cut a thin slice off the base of each shell so that it will stand firmly. Set aside.

2 Preheat the oven to 200°C (400°F/Gas 6). Put the couscous in a bowl. Add ⅓ cup (80 ml/2½ fl oz) of the lemon juice, the spices, 3 cups (750 ml/26 fl oz) of the stock, apricots and mint. Mix well, then leave to soak for 10 minutes, or until all the stock has been absorbed.

3 Rinse the turkey inside and out, then pat dry with paper towels. Place the turkey, breast side down, on a wire rack in a roasting pan and pour in 150 ml (5 fl oz) hot water. Use a spoon to loosely stuff some of the couscous into the neck end of the turkey. Secure the skin flap underneath the bird with the wing tips. Spoon 2 tablespoons of the remaining lemon juice over the bird.

4 Cover the turkey loosely with foil and roast for 1¼ hours, basting with the pan juices occasionally to keep it moist. Meanwhile, fill the lemon halves with some of the remaining couscous, pressing down gently and mounding up the top. Spread the rest of the couscous in a small ovenproof dish and sit the lemon halves on top. Cover loosely with foil.

5 Remove the foil from the turkey, roast for 10 minutes, then baste. Place the couscous dish in the oven and roast the turkey for another 20 minutes, or until the juices run clear when a skewer is inserted into the thickest part of the thigh.

6 Remove the turkey to a carving board, cover loosely with foil to keep warm, and set aside to rest for 10 minutes. Meanwhile, skim the fat from the pan juices, then add the sherry and remaining stock. Place the pan on the stove top and bring to a boil, scraping up all the browned bits from the bottom of the pan. Allow to boil for 5 minutes, then season to taste with salt and black pepper.

7 Carve the turkey and serve with the gravy, extra couscous and the couscous-filled lemons, garnished with mint sprigs.

Cook's tip

Keep the turkey carcass to make stock for soup. Place the carcass with some onion, carrot, celery tops and herbs in enough water to cover. Simmer for 3–4 hours, then strain and slowly reduce the liquid.

Turkey drumsticks with baby vegetables

This is a simple dish to prepare and makes an economical and healthy meal. Roasted in the French style — in stock with a few herbs — the meat becomes wonderfully moist and tender. Serve with baked potatoes.

2 tablespoons sunflower oil
4 leeks, white part only, thickly sliced
12 baby carrots
12 baby zucchini (courgettes)
12 baby corn
300 ml (10 fl oz) turkey or chicken stock
2 sprigs fresh rosemary
1 bay leaf
2 large turkey drumsticks, about 500 g (1 lb) each, skinned
freshly ground black pepper

Serves 4
Preparation 10 minutes
Cooking 1½ hours

1 Preheat the oven to 200°C (400°F/Gas 6). Heat the oil in a large flameproof casserole dish over medium–high heat. Add the leeks, carrots, zucchini and baby corn and sauté for 3–4 minutes, until beginning to brown.

2 Pour in the stock and add the rosemary sprigs and bay leaf. Rinse the drumsticks, then pat dry with paper towels. Season the drumsticks with pepper and place on top of the vegetables.

3 Transfer to the oven and cook for about 1½ hours, basting the turkey with the pan juices about halfway through, and stirring the vegetables so they cook evenly. The turkey should be golden brown, and the juices should run clear when a skewer is inserted into the thickest part of a drumstick.

4 Carve the meat from the drumsticks into slices. Serve with the vegetables and a little of the pan juices spooned over.

Roast turkey with celery sauce

The turkey in this recipe is partly boned, leaving the wings and legs attached, so that when the bird is remoulded before cooking it closely resembles its original shape.

1 turkey, about 3.5 kg (7 lb), with giblets reserved for stock
15 g (½ oz) butter, softened
250 g (9 oz) bacon slices, rind removed
celery leaves and walnut halves, to garnish

CELERY STUFFING
See page 146

CELERY SAUCE
15 g (½ oz) butter
3 small celery stalks, cut into very fine strips
½ teaspoon celery seeds
¼ cup (35 g/1 oz) plain (all-purpose) flour
2 cups (500 ml/17 fl oz) chicken stock
3 tablespoons dry sherry

Serves 6–8
Preparation 1 hour
Cooking 3¼ hours

1 Rinse the turkey inside and out, then pat dry with paper towels. Place on a chopping board, breast side down. Using a very sharp knife, make a deep incision along the centre of the backbone, cutting right down to the bone. Starting at one side, insert the knife under the skin and flesh and, with small cutting strokes, gradually cut the flesh away from the carcass. Keep the knife close to the bone at all times and work from the backbone down to the tip of the breastbone.

2 When the knife comes into contact with the thigh, work around the ball and socket joint and gently pull it free from the main carcass. Do the same with the wing joint. On reaching the tip of the breastbone, turn the turkey around and repeat along the other side. Finally, work the knife carefully along the tip of the breastbone to free it completely, taking care not to cut through the skin, which is very thin at this point. Set the turkey aside, then prepare the Celery stuffing (see page 146).

3 Preheat the oven to 220°C (425°F/Gas 7). Place the turkey, breast side down, on the work surface and open it out flat. Spoon the stuffing along the centre, then bring the sides and neck flap neatly back over the stuffing. Using kitchen string, sew the turkey together to enclose the stuffing. Turn the bird over and mould it back into its original shape. Tuck the wings underneath and tie the legs together. Put the turkey in a roasting pan, rub it all over with the butter, then cover it with the bacon slices. Cover the pan with foil, tucking it securely under the rim.

4 Roast for 50 minutes, then reduce the oven temperature to 180°C (350°F/Gas 4). Roast, basting frequently with the pan juices, for another 1 hour. Remove the foil and bacon and roast the turkey, basting often, for a further 30 minutes to 1 hour, or until the juices run clear when a skewer is inserted into the thickest part of the thigh. (Loosely cover the turkey with foil if it starts to brown too quickly.) Crumble the bacon into small pieces and set aside in a warm place.

5 Meanwhile, start making the celery sauce. Melt the butter in a saucepan, add the celery and celery seeds and sauté gently for 5 minutes, or until the celery has softened. Remove from the heat and set aside.

6 Carefully remove the turkey to a warmed serving plate. Cover loosely with foil to keep warm, and set aside to rest while you finish making the sauce.

7 Skim all but about 2 tablespoons of the fat from the pan juices. Place the pan on the stovetop over medium heat. Add the flour and stir until smooth, then cook, stirring, for 1–2 minutes. Add the stock and bring to a boil, scraping up all the browned bits from the bottom of the pan. Strain the sauce into the sautéed celery mixture and add the sherry. Stir well, season to taste with salt and pepper and simmer for 5 minutes.

8 Garnish the turkey generously with celery leaves and walnut halves. Scatter with the reserved crispy bacon, then carve and serve with the celery sauce.

Roast duckling à l'orange

The enduring popularity of this French classic is well-deserved: the bright tang of citrus cuts beautifully through the richness of the duck. The flavour is quite special.

1 duckling, about 2 kg (4 lb)
salt and freshly ground black pepper
1 lemon, pricked well with a fork
6 cloves garlic, unpeeled
2 bay leaves
zest of 1 orange, finely slivered
⅓ cup (80 ml/2½ fl oz) white wine vinegar
¼ cup (55 g/2 oz) sugar
⅔ cup (170 ml/5½ fl oz) orange juice
1¾ cups (435 ml/15 fl oz) chicken stock
1 teaspoon tomato paste (concentrated purée)
½ cup (125 ml/4 fl oz) dry white wine
2 teaspoons cornflour (cornstarch), mixed to a paste with 2 tablespoons cold water

Serves 4
Preparation 15 minutes
Cooking 1¾ hours

1 Preheat the oven to 230°C (450°F/Gas 8). Rinse the duck inside and out, pat dry with paper towels, then remove and discard the fat from the body cavity. Prick the skin all over with a fork. Season the cavity with salt and black pepper. Insert the lemon, garlic and bay leaves inside the duck.

2 Place the duck, breast side up, on a wire rack in a roasting pan. Season well. Roast, uncovered, for 45 minutes, spooning off the fat as it accumulates. Reduce the oven temperature to 180°C (350°F/Gas 4) and continue roasting for another 35–45 minutes, until the juices run slightly pink when a skewer is inserted into the thigh.

3 While the duck is roasting, cook the orange zest for 10 minutes in a small saucepan of boiling water; drain and set aside. Meanwhile, boil the vinegar and sugar without stirring in a saucepan over medium heat, for about 4 minutes, until the mixture turns an amber colour. Stir in the orange juice, stock, tomato paste and reserved orange zest; season well and set aside.

4 Remove the duck to a carving board, cover loosely with foil to keep warm, and set aside to rest. To make the sauce, skim the fat from the roasting pan, pour in the wine and boil on the stovetop for 2 minutes, scraping up all the browned bits. Add to the orange juice mixture and cook, uncovered, for about 10 minutes, until reduced by one-third. Blend in the cornflour mixture and stir constantly for 3 minutes, until the mixture thickens. Carve the duck. Serve drizzled with the orange sauce.

Roast duck with redcurrant sauce

The rich, deep flavour of roasted duck is enhanced by the piquancy of the redcurrant sauce. For a sumptuous meal, serve with steamed potatoes, broccoli, asparagus and carrots.

1 duck, about 2.5 kg (5 lb)

REDCURRANT SAUCE
30 g (1 oz) butter
2 French shallots, finely chopped
1 clove garlic, finely chopped
2 tablespoons balsamic vinegar
½ cup (125 ml/4 fl oz) red wine
2 sprigs fresh thyme or rosemary
1 teaspoon tomato paste (concentrated purée)
½ cup (60 g/2 oz) redcurrants or 3 tablespoons redcurrant jelly
¼ cup (40 g/1½ oz) blueberries (optional)
redcurrants, to garnish (optional)

Serves 4–6
Preparation 15 minutes
Cooking 1¾ hours

1 Preheat the oven to 230°C (450°F/Gas 8). Rinse the duck inside and out, then pat dry with paper towels. Use kitchen string to tie the legs firmly together, then place the duck on a wire rack in a roasting pan. Prick the skin all over to allow the fat to drain off.

2 Roast the duck for 1¾ hours, spooning the excess fat from the roasting pan twice during cooking. Remove the duck to a carving board, cover loosely with foil to keep warm, and set aside to rest while making the redcurrant sauce.

3 Melt the butter in a saucepan over high heat. Add the shallots and garlic and sauté for 2 minutes. Add the vinegar, wine, herb sprigs and tomato paste. Cook for 30 seconds, reduce the heat to low, add the redcurrants or redcurrant jelly, and blueberries if using, and simmer for 2 minutes.

4 To carve the duck, turn it onto its breast and carve down both sides of the backbone. Discard the backbone. Cut off the legs, then cut the breast meat away from the breastbone, keeping the knife close to the bone. Cut the leg in two between the thigh and the drumstick. Cut the breast in two.

5 Slice the duck and serve with steamed vegetables, drizzled with the redcurrant sauce, and garnished with redcurrants, if using.

Boned stuffed duck

Stuffed with an enticing combination of dried apricots and cherries soaked in orange juice, this boned duck recipe makes a delectable dinner party dish. Serve with potatoes and crisp greens.

½ cup (90 g/3 oz) dried apricots, chopped
⅓ cup (60 g/2 oz) dried cherries
½ cup (125 ml/4 fl oz) orange juice
½ cup (90 g/3 oz) wild rice
2 tablespoons vegetable oil
6 spring onions (scallions), sliced
2 cloves garlic, chopped
75 g (2½ oz) dark flat mushrooms, chopped
1 duck, about 2 kg (4 lb), boned, and its liver chopped
500 g (1 lb) finely minced (ground) pork or veal
3 tablespoons chopped fresh thyme and parsley
pinch of ground allspice
⅓ cup (80 ml/2½ fl oz) brandy
salt and freshly ground black pepper
1 egg, beaten
100 g (3½ oz) butter, melted

Serves 4–6
Preparation 30 minutes + 1 hour soaking
Cooking 2½ hours

1 In a large bowl, soak the apricots and cherries in the orange juice for 1 hour. Meanwhile, cook the rice in a saucepan of boiling water for 45 minutes, or until tender. Drain, rinse and leave to cool.

2 Heat the oil in a small saucepan. Add the spring onions and garlic and sauté over medium heat for 3–4 minutes, until soft. Add the mushrooms and the duck liver and sauté for 2–3 minutes, or until soft. Remove from the heat and allow to cool.

3 Preheat the oven to 180°C (350°F/Gas 4). Add the mushroom mixture to the soaked dried fruit, along with the rice, pork or veal, herbs, allspice and brandy. Mix together well. Check the seasoning of the stuffing by frying a small patty of the mixture, then tasting it. Season the stuffing with salt and black pepper and just enough egg to bind the mixture.

4 Rinse the duck, then pat dry with paper towels. Place the boned duck on a chopping board, skin side down. Place the stuffing down the centre of the bird. Fold over the sides of the bird to form a neat roll, then sew it together with a trussing needle and kitchen string, or a needle and strong thread.

5 Soak a large piece of muslin (cheesecloth) in the melted butter. Wrap it tightly around the duck, tying both ends so that it looks like a Christmas cracker. Place the duck on a wire rack in a roasting pan and roast for 1¼ hours, basting frequently with the pan juices. Remove the cloth to help brown the skin, then roast for a further 15 minutes.

6 Remove the duck to a carving board, cover loosely with foil to keep warm, and set aside to rest for 15 minutes. Serve hot, carved into thick slices, or allow to cool, then refrigerate before slicing.

Fish

Coriander salmon parcels

Cooking fish in foil is an ideal way to retain all its flavour and nutrients. Luscious salmon fillets are infused with fragrant flavours drawn from South-east Asia, complementing their gentle richness.

½ cup (125 ml/4 fl oz) coconut milk
1 tablespoon fish sauce
1 teaspoon sesame oil
150 g (5 oz) baby English spinach leaves
4 x 200 g (7 oz) salmon fillets
2 limes, cut into 1 cm (½ inch) rounds
4 fresh makrut (kaffir lime) leaves, cut into slivers
1 large red chilli, finely sliced (optional)
¾ cup (25 g/1 oz) fresh coriander (cilantro) leaves
½ cup (25 g/1 oz) fresh Thai basil
2 spring onions (scallions), finely sliced
½ cup (70 g/2½ oz) chopped cashew nuts, toasted (optional)

Serves 4
Preparation 20 minutes
Cooking 12 minutes

1 Preheat the oven to 180°C (350°F/Gas 4). Combine the coconut milk, fish sauce and sesame oil in a small bowl.

2 Lay four 30 cm (12 inch) squares of foil on a work surface. Divide the spinach among the foil squares. Place a salmon fillet in the centre of each square; top each fillet with some of the lime rounds, makrut leaves, chilli (if using), coriander, basil and spring onion.

3 Fold in two opposite sides of each foil square, forming a seam down the middle. Fold over the bottom end several times to secure. At the open end of each parcel, pour in 2 tablespoons of the coconut milk mixture; fold and secure both top ends.

4 Place the parcels on a baking tray and bake for about 12 minutes for medium–rare salmon, or until cooked to your liking. Serve the fish in the parcels, with steamed vegetables and rice. Garnish with cashews, if desired.

Whole baked fish with chermoula

Sea bass makes an impressive meal and its delicious flesh is moist, tender and sweet. Here it's stuffed with chermoula – an exotic, Moroccan-style fresh herb and spice mixture – then braised on a bed of vegetables.

1 whole sea bass or other firm white fish, about 1 kg (2 lb), cleaned
salt and freshly ground black pepper
175 g (6 oz) thin green beans, halved
500 g (1 lb) roasting (floury) potatoes, peeled
2 spring onions (scallions), finely chopped
250 g (9 oz) grape or cherry tomatoes
⅓ cup (50 g/1¾ oz) pitted black olives
300 ml (10 fl oz) fish stock, hot

CHERMOULA
4 cloves garlic
1 small red chilli, seeded
1 cup (30 g/1 oz) fresh coriander (cilantro) leaves
1 teaspoon paprika
½ teaspoon ground cumin
¼ cup (60 ml/2 fl oz) vegetable oil
1 lemon, juiced

Serves 4
Preparation 20 minutes + marinating
Cooking 55 minutes

1 Cut about six deep, diagonal slashes in the flesh on each side of the fish. Place the fish in a wide, non-metallic dish.

2 Put the chermoula ingredients in a food processor or blender and process until finely chopped and well combined. Season to taste with salt and black pepper. Spread about half the chermoula inside the fish and into the slashes. Cover and refrigerate the fish and the remaining chermoula, allowing the fish to marinate for at least 30 minutes.

3 Preheat the oven to 200°C (400°F/Gas 6). Drop the beans into a saucepan of boiling water and blanch for 1 minute, then drain and refresh in cold water. Thinly slice the potatoes and spread in a shallow layer with the spring onions in a wide, deep baking dish. Scatter the beans, tomatoes and olives over the top.

4 Pour the stock over the vegetables and place the fish on top. Cover with foil and bake for 40–50 minutes, until the potatoes are tender and the fish flakes easily when tested with a fork. Serve the whole fish with the vegetables on a platter, with the reserved chermoula as a sauce.

Baked fish and vegetable parcels

Halibut has a firm, melt-in-your-mouth texture; it is beautifully fresh and white. If you can't find halibut, substitute another firm-fleshed fish such as sea bass, cod, sole, snapper or swordfish.

500 g (1 lb) halibut steak, cut into 4 pieces, or use other thick white fish steaks
salt and freshly ground black pepper
4 teaspoons lemon juice
2 shallots, finely chopped
4 tablespoons butter, cut into cubes
2 carrots, peeled and julienned
1 red capsicum (bell pepper), cut into thin strips
1 green capsicum (bell pepper), cut into thin strips

Serves 4
Preparation 30 minutes
Cooking 15 minutes

1 Preheat the oven to 250°C (480°F/Gas 9). Cut out four sheets of baking (parchment) paper or foil, each measuring about 30 x 46 cm (12 x 18 inches). Place a piece of fish on each sheet, parallel to a narrow side, about 7.5 cm (3 inches) from the edge. Arrange remaining ingredients on top, distributing them equally.

2 Fold the baking paper or foil over the fish, seal the edges tightly and place on a baking tray. Bake for about 15 minutes, until the baking paper puffs out.

3 Place each parcel on a serving plate and cut a slit on top of each. Open them out carefully (the steam will be hot) and serve.

Cook's tip

Cooking in parcels is called *en papillote*, meaning in paper casing. Halibut cooks up beautifully by this method. Also try cod, salmon, sole, and any firm-fleshed fish that can be cut into chunks or pieces.

Baked fish with stuffing

Striped bass is a beautifully coloured fish with a mild, sweet flavour and a moist, flaky white flesh. If you can't obtain any, try this recipe with other firm-fleshed white fish such as snapper.

olive oil spray
1 striped bass or other white fish, about 680 g (1½ lb), cleaned, butterflied, boned and opened flat, with the head and tail left on
1 tablespoon lemon juice

Serves 2
Preparation 25 minutes
Cooking 20 minutes

STUFFING
3 tablespoons chopped fresh parsley
3 tablespoons grated parmesan
1 cup (100 g/3½ oz) dry breadcrumbs
1 teaspoon dried thyme, crumbled
4 tablespoons melted butter
salt and freshly ground black pepper

1 Preheat the oven to 200°C (400°F/Gas 6). Lightly coat a 25 x 38 cm (10 x 15 inch) baking tray with olive oil spray.

2 Rub the inside of the fish with the lemon juice. Place the fish on the baking tray, skin side down, with the cavity open.

3 Mix all the stuffing ingredients together in a small bowl. Press the stuffing mixture evenly into the open cavity. Bake, uncovered, for 15–20 minutes, until the topping is golden and the fish flakes easily when tested with a fork.

Cook's tip

To stuff a butterflied fish, open the fish flat on a baking tray and heap each side with stuffing. Bake the fish opened flat.

Crumbed fish with oven-baked wedges

You can enjoy this light, guilt-free version of fish and chips without worrying about the fat content – the secret to the golden wedges is to coat them with egg white, not oil. The herbs make the crumb coating extra special.

750 g (1 lb 10 oz) roasting (floury) potatoes, peeled
olive oil spray
1 egg white
4 firm white fish fillets, about 150 g (5 oz) each
4 teaspoons mayonnaise or aïoli
¾ cup (60 g/2 oz) fresh white breadcrumbs
1 tablespoon butter, melted
3 teaspoons grated parmesan
1 tablespoon chopped fresh chives
1 tablespoon chopped fresh flat-leaf parsley, plus extra sprigs to garnish
salt and freshly ground black pepper
lemon wedges, to serve

Serves 4
Preparation 20 minutes
Cooking 45 minutes

1 Preheat the oven to 200°C (400°F/Gas 6). Cook the potatoes in a saucepan of boiling water for 5 minutes. Drain, then dry thoroughly with paper towels. Cut each potato lengthwise into slices about 2 cm (¾ inch) thick, then cut each slice into two or three thick wedges.

2 Lightly coat a non-stick baking tray with olive oil spray. In a bowl, beat the egg white until frothy. Toss the potato wedges in the egg white, gently shake off any excess, then spread them out on the baking tray. Bake for 20 minutes.

3 Meanwhile, prepare the fish. Lightly coat another non-stick baking tray with olive oil spray. Place the fish fillets, skin side down, on the baking tray and spread 1 teaspoon mayonnaise or aïoli over each fillet. Mix together the breadcrumbs, butter, parmesan, chives and parsley and season with salt and black pepper. Spread the crumb mixture evenly over the fillets, pressing it on gently.

4 Turn the potato wedges over and place the fish on the top shelf of the oven. Bake for 10–15 minutes, or until the wedges are cooked and golden, and the fish flakes easily when tested with a fork. Divide the fish and chips among serving plates, garnish with parsley sprigs and serve with lemon wedges.

Indian-style fish

Coconut milk adds a creamy richness to the fish fillets, keeping them beautifully moist; and mint and ginger lend some freshness and zing. Zucchinis and minted new potatoes are served alongside.

1 kg (2 lb) small unpeeled new potatoes
2 zucchini (courgettes), cut into large dice
4 plaice, sole or trout fillets, or thin white fish fillets, about 150 g (5 oz) each
salt and freshly ground black pepper
2 cm (¾ inch) piece fresh ginger, peeled and finely chopped
½ red onion, finely chopped
1 mild red chilli, seeded and finely chopped
⅓ cup (80 ml/2½ fl oz) coconut milk
4 tablespoons chopped fresh mint
1 tablespoon sesame seeds
2 teaspoons yellow mustard seeds
2 teaspoons soy sauce

Serves 4
Preparation 20 minutes
Cooking 25 minutes

1 Preheat the oven to 180°C (350°F/Gas 4).

2 Cook the potatoes in a saucepan of boiling water for 10 minutes, then put the zucchini in a steamer above the potatoes and cook for another 4 minutes, or until the potatoes and zucchini are tender. Drain the vegetables and keep warm.

3 Meanwhile, cut out four large sheets of baking (parchment) paper or foil, each large enough to enclose a fish fillet. Lay a fillet on each sheet and season with salt and black pepper. In a bowl, mix together the ginger, onion, chilli, coconut milk and half the mint, then spread over the fish. Fold over the paper or foil, then pleat or twist the ends to seal securely. Put the parcels on a large baking tray and bake for 10–12 minutes, or until the fish flakes easily when tested with a fork.

4 Heat a dry frying pan over medium heat. Add the sesame seeds and mustard seeds, then cover and fry for 2–3 minutes, or until lightly toasted, shaking the pan frequently. Take the pan off the heat, stir in the soy sauce, then cover and set aside until the seeds stop 'popping'. Stir the zucchini into the seed mixture.

5 Toss the potatoes with the remaining mint. Arrange the fish parcels on serving plates and serve with the zucchini and potatoes.

Red mullet parcels with orange

This beautiful fish has lean, firm flesh that tastes almost like shellfish. Whole red mullet are baked on a bed of fennel and orange segments and are wonderful simply served with new potatoes and steamed green beans.

2 tablespoons olive oil
2 large fennel bulbs, halved and very thinly sliced
2 cloves garlic, chopped
8 spring onions (scallions), cut into short lengths
3 small oranges
salt and freshly ground black pepper
4 red mullet, about 200 g (7 oz) each, scaled and gutted; remove the heads if you wish

Serves 4
Preparation 15 minutes
Cooking 20 minutes

1 Preheat the oven to 220°C (425°F/Gas 7). Heat the olive oil in a saucepan, add the fennel, garlic and spring onions and sauté over medium heat for 5 minutes, or until softened.

2 Meanwhile, squeeze the juice from one of the oranges into a bowl. Cut the peel and pith from the other two oranges. Holding each orange over the bowl to catch the juices, cut between the membranes to release the segments.

3 Divide the fennel mixture and orange segments among four large sheets of baking (parchment) paper or foil. Slash each fish three or four times on both sides, then place on top of the fennel and orange. Sprinkle with the orange juice and season with salt and black pepper.

4 Wrap the paper or foil around each fish and fold over to seal each parcel. Place the parcels on a baking tray and bake for 12–15 minutes, until the fish flakes easily when tested with a fork.

5 Leaving the parcels sealed, present them on individual serving plates so they can be opened at the table.

Vegetables

Baked jacket potatoes

4 large roasting (floury) potatoes, unpeeled
vegetable oil, for brushing

Serves 4
Preparation 5 minutes
Cooking 1 hour

1 Preheat the oven to 200°C (400°F/Gas 6). Wash the potatoes and dry thoroughly with paper towels.

2 Brush four squares of foil with some oil and use these to loosely wrap the potatoes. Place the potatoes on a baking tray and bake for about 1 hour, then remove from the oven.

3 Carefully open the foil parcels. Using a sharp knife, cut a deep cross into each potato. Gently push the flesh outward with two forks. Serve the potatoes with butter, sour cream and fresh chives, or the topping of your choice.

Roast potatoes

1 kg (2 lb) new potatoes, unpeeled
2 tablespoons vegetable oil
1–2 tablespoons fresh thyme
1 tablespoon fresh rosemary leaves
coarse sea salt

Serves 4
Preparation 5 minutes
Cooking 30 minutes

1 Preheat the oven to 200°C (400°F/Gas 6). Wash the potatoes and dry thoroughly with paper towels, then cut in halves lengthwise.

2 Brush a baking tray with the oil and sprinkle with the herbs and some salt. Place the potatoes cut side down on the tray and bake for about 30 minutes. Serve with sour cream or crème fraîche.

Fan potatoes

40 g (1 ½ oz) butter, melted, plus extra for brushing
8 boiling (waxy) potatoes
salt and freshly ground black pepper

Serves 4
Preparation 15 minutes
Cooking 50 minutes

1 Preheat the oven to 200°C (400°F/Gas 6). Brush a baking dish with melted butter. Peel and wash the potatoes and dry thoroughly with paper towels. Without cutting all the way through them, use a sharp knife to slice the potatoes at 3 mm (⅛ inch) intervals.

2 Place the potatoes in the baking dish with the sliced sides facing upwards. Brush with melted butter and season with salt and black pepper. Bake for about 50 minutes, until golden, occasionally basting with butter from the bottom of the dish. Serve with a mixed leaf salad with vinaigrette or yogurt dressing.

Potato gratin

melted butter, for brushing
750 g (1 lb 10 oz) all-purpose potatoes
salt and freshly ground black pepper
pinch of freshly grated nutmeg
200 ml (7 fl oz) whipping cream
¼ (60 ml/2 fl oz) milk
2 tablespoons grated emmenthal or Swiss cheese

Serves 4
Preparation 20 minutes
Cooking 45 minutes

1 Preheat the oven to 200°C (400°F/Gas 6). Brush a baking dish with melted butter. Peel and wash the potatoes, dry thoroughly with paper towels, then cut into thin slices using a sharp knife or a mandoline.

2 Layer the potatoes in the baking dish, overlapping the slices, and season with some salt, black pepper and nutmeg. Combine the cream and milk and pour over the potatoes. Sprinkle with the cheese and bake for about 45 minutes, until golden. Serve hot, with meat dishes or a salad.

Twice-baked stuffed sweet potatoes

Like potatoes, sweet potatoes are delicious when baked. They have a sweet taste and when mashed are beautifully smooth. They are a great accompaniment to roasted meats.

2 large orange sweet potatoes
225 g (8 oz) can crushed pineapple
1 tablespoon vegetable oil
1 tablespoon butter
1 tablespoon soft brown sugar
1 teaspoon grated orange zest
½ teaspoon salt
pecans, for sprinkling

Serves 4
Preparation 20 minutes
Cooking 1 hour 20 minutes

1 Preheat the oven to 180°C (350°F/Gas 4). Pierce each sweet potato twice with the tip of a sharp knife. Place on a baking tray and bake for about 50 minutes, until soft. Set aside until the sweet potatoes are cool enough to handle but still very warm.

2 Reduce the oven temperature to 160°C (320°F/Gas 2–3). Cut the sweet potatoes in half lengthwise. Scoop out the flesh and place in a bowl, being careful not to tear the skin. Reserve the skins.

3 To the sweet potato flesh, add the pineapple, oil, butter, sugar, orange zest and salt. Beat with electric beaters or a whisk until slightly fluffy.

4 Place the sweet potato skins on a baking tray and fill with the sweet potato mixture, mounding it a little. Bake for 15 minutes, then sprinkle with the pecans and bake for a final 15 minutes.

Cook's tip

This recipe can be made up to a day ahead. Bake and stuff the sweet potatoes as directed. Place in a shallow dish, cover loosely with plastic wrap and refrigerate. Remove from the refrigerator 30 minutes before baking and bake as directed.

Spiced garlic and ginger potatoes

Crisp and golden outside, light and fluffy inside, roast potatoes are the classic accompaniment to a roast. The combination of ginger and garlic adds a delicious spiciness that is sure to please.

3 cm (1 inch) unpeeled piece of fresh ginger
750 g (1 lb 10 oz) unpeeled small new potatoes
1 tablespoon olive oil
8 unpeeled cloves garlic
1½ teaspoons fennel seeds
1½ teaspoons cumin seeds
1½ teaspoons ground turmeric
1 tablespoon lemon juice
salt

Serves 4
Preparation 5 minutes
Cooking 40 minutes

1 Preheat the oven to 200°C (400°F/Gas 6). Cut the ginger into three slices and the potatoes into chunks.

2 Heat the olive oil in a large non-stick frying pan. Sauté the ginger with the garlic cloves, fennel seeds, cumin seeds and turmeric for 1 minute. Add the potatoes and sauté for 5 minutes, or until golden brown.

3 Transfer the mixture to a roasting pan, pour in 100 ml (3½ fl oz) water, then bake for 25–30 minutes, or until the potatoes are well browned and the liquid has evaporated, turning the potatoes occasionally.

4 Discard the ginger. Squeeze the garlic out of the cloves onto the potatoes, drizzle with the lemon juice and season with salt. Serve hot.

Cook's tip

Instead of garlic cloves, you can also use garlic chives. Snip the stalks into short lengths and sprinkle over the potatoes just before serving.

Roast new potatoes with thyme

2 tablespoons olive oil
500 g (1 lb) unpeeled small new potatoes
coarse sea salt
2 tablespoons fresh thyme

Serves 4
Preparation 5 minutes
Cooking 35 minutes

1 Preheat the oven to 230°C (450°F/Gas 8). Pour the olive oil into a large, shallow baking dish and place in the oven to heat.

2 Meanwhile, cook the potatoes in a large saucepan of boiling water for 5 minutes, then drain well.

3 Remove the baking dish from the oven and add the potatoes to the hot oil; they should sizzle. Stir well to coat in the hot oil, then sprinkle with salt and thyme. Roast on the top shelf of the oven for 20 minutes, until golden.

Minted peas

500 g (1 lb) peas in the pod
2 sprigs fresh mint or 1 tablespoon chopped mint
1 tablespoon butter
salt and freshly ground black pepper
pinch of caster (superfine) sugar

Serves 4
Preparation 20 minutes
Cooking 15 minutes

1 Remove the peas from their pods. Pick the mint leaves from the sprigs, finely shred the leaves and set aside. Trim the ends of the stalks.

2 Bring a saucepan of water to a boil over medium heat. Add the mint stalks and peas and cook for 10 minutes, or until the peas are tender. Drain, discarding the mint stalks.

3 Return the peas to the pan with the butter and chopped mint. Season with salt and black pepper and add the sugar. Toss over low heat until the butter has melted. Serve immediately.

Glazed carrots

3 carrots
1 tablespoon butter
1 tablespoon honey
salt

Serves 6
Preparation 10 minutes
Cooking 10 minutes

1 Peel the carrots and cut into thin slices on a slight diagonal. Cook in a saucepan of boiling water over medium heat for 5 minutes, or until just tender. Drain.

2 Add the butter and honey to the pan. Cook over low heat, stirring and tossing, for 2 minutes, or until the carrots are well glazed. Season with a pinch of salt and serve.

Creamed spinach

2 bunches (about 1 kg/2 lb) English spinach
1 tablespoon butter
2 cloves garlic, crushed
½ cup (125 ml/4 fl oz) whipping cream
pinch of freshly ground nutmeg
salt and freshly ground black pepper

Serves 4
Preparation 15 minutes
Cooking 5 minutes

1 Pull the spinach leaves from the stems and immerse them in a large bowl of cold water. Leave for 5 minutes, then lift from the water (any dirt will have sunk to the bottom). Drain well, then dry in a salad spinner or a clean tea towel (dish towel) to remove as much water as possible. Finely shred the leaves.

2 Melt the butter in a large frying pan over medium heat. Add the garlic and sauté for 1 minute, then pour in the cream. Bring to a boil, then add the spinach and cook until wilted and soft. Season with nutmeg, salt and black pepper and serve.

Roasted vegetables

Autumn and winter vegetables are great for roasting. Vary the ingredients depending on what looks appealing and good value on the day. Serve with roast poultry or meat or in generous quantities as a stand-alone dish.

2 tablespoons olive oil
6 cloves garlic, sliced
500 g (1 lb) butternut pumpkin (squash), peeled and cut into chunks
300 g (10 oz) brussels sprouts, trimmed and halved
2 large red apples, quartered, cored and thickly sliced
¼ cup (35 g/1 oz) sun-dried tomatoes, drained if in oil, and thinly sliced
2 rosemary sprigs or 1 teaspoon dried rosemary
pinch of salt
250 g (9 oz) portobello or Swiss brown mushrooms, halved
3 tablespoons grated parmesan or mature cheddar (optional)

Serves 4
Preparation 20 minutes
Cooking 40–45 minutes

1 Preheat the oven to 200°C (400°F/Gas 6). Put the olive oil and garlic in a large roasting pan and heat for 3 minutes in the oven.

2 Remove the pan from the oven and add the pumpkin, brussels sprouts, apples, sun-dried tomatoes and rosemary. Sprinkle with salt and toss to combine.

3 Roast for 20 minutes, turning the vegetables halfway through. Add the mushrooms, toss with the other vegetables, then roast for a further 15 minutes, or until the vegetables are golden and tender.

4 If you are using cheese, sprinkle it over the top and roast for a further 5 minutes. Serve immediately.

Cook's tip

You could make this dish with parsnip, carrot, swede (rutabaga) or turnip instead of the pumpkin, or throw in some baby onions — whatever takes your fancy. For a special occasion, use thickly sliced fresh shiitake mushrooms in place of the portobello or Swiss brown varieties.

Roasted vegetable crumble

Sweetly flavoured, roasted vegetables topped with a savoury crumble are irresistible. Other root vegetables, such as parsnips and carrots, are also very good in this dish.

6 small red onions, quartered
400 g (14 oz) orange sweet potato, peeled and cut into chunks
2 tablespoons olive oil
1 clove garlic, crushed
1 teaspoon fresh thyme
2 large zucchini (courgettes), cut into slices
100 g (3½ oz) baby button mushrooms
350 g (12 oz) roma (plum) tomatoes, quartered

Serves 4
Preparation 20 minutes
Cooking 1 hour 20 minutes

CRUMBLE TOPPING
½ cup (75 g/2½ oz) wholemeal (whole-wheat) flour
25 g (1 oz) chilled butter, diced
1 tablespoon chilled water
⅔ cup (75 g/2½ oz) fresh wholemeal (whole-wheat) breadcrumbs
½ cup (50 g/1¾ oz) grated parmesan
3 tablespoons mixed chopped nuts
2 tablespoons sunflower seeds
2 tablespoons pepitas (pumpkin seeds)
1 teaspoon fresh thyme

1 Preheat the oven to 190°C (375°F/Gas 5). Put a baking dish or roasting pan measuring about 30 x 20 x 4 cm (12 x 8 x 1½ inches) in the oven and allow it to heat for 10 minutes.

2 Put the onions and sweet potatoes in a bowl, drizzle with 1 tablespoon of the olive oil and gently toss to coat. Place in the heated dish and roast for 30 minutes, turning the vegetables halfway through. In the same bowl, mix the remaining oil with the garlic and thyme. Add the zucchini, mushrooms and tomatoes and gently toss to coat. Add to the other vegetables and roast for 20 minutes more.

3 Meanwhile, make the crumble topping. Put the flour in a bowl and rub in the butter using your fingertips. Add the water and mix together with a fork to make large crumbs. Stir in the remaining crumble ingredients.

4 Sprinkle the crumble mixture over the vegetables. Bake for 15–20 minutes, or until the topping is golden brown and all the vegetables are tender. Remove from the oven and leave to stand for 3–4 minutes before serving.

Mediterranean stuffed vegetables

This colourful array of oven-cooked stuffed vegetables makes an appetising main dish, ideal for an informal help-yourself meal. Use a combination of red, yellow and green capsicums. Serve warm or cool, sprinkled with basil.

½ cup (100 g/3½ oz) long-grain white rice
250 g (9 oz) lean minced (ground) lamb
1 onion, chopped
4 capsicums (bell peppers)
4 large firm but ripe tomatoes
2 large zucchini (courgettes), about 225 g (8 oz) each
1 tablespoon olive oil
3 cloves garlic, chopped
170 g (6 oz) baby English spinach leaves
2 tablespoons shredded fresh basil, plus extra, to garnish
1 egg, lightly beaten
salt and freshly ground black pepper

Serves 4
Preparation 45 minutes
Cooking 1 hour

1 Cook the rice in a saucepan of boiling water for 10–12 minutes, or according to the packet instructions, until tender. Drain. Meanwhile, put the lamb and onion in a non-stick frying pan and fry until the lamb is lightly browned and cooked through and the onion has softened, breaking up the meat so it browns evenly. Set aside.

2 Cut each capsicum in half lengthwise through the stalk and remove the seeds and membranes. Cut the tops (stalk end) off the tomatoes and hollow out the insides. Chop the tops and hollowed-out flesh and place in a bowl with any tomato juices. Cut the zucchini in half lengthwise and hollow out the centres to leave shells 5 mm (¼ inch) thick. Chop the hollowed-out zucchini flesh and add it to the chopped tomatoes.

3 Preheat the oven to 180°C (350°F/Gas 4). Heat the olive oil in a non-stick frying pan, add the garlic and chopped vegetables and cook, stirring, until they soften slightly. Add the baby spinach and cook over medium heat for a minute or so until wilted. Remove from the heat and add the basil, rice and lamb. Add the egg, season with salt and black pepper and mix well.

4 Spoon the stuffing into the capsicum, tomato and zucchini shells. Arrange the capsicums and zucchini in a single layer in one or two roasting pans – not too crowded together. Cover with foil and roast for 15 minutes. Add the tomatoes and continue roasting for 15 minutes, or until the vegetables are almost tender. Remove the foil and roast for a further 15–20 minutes.

Roast vegetables with pears

A warming autumnal dish of roasted root vegetables and fragrant pears. The addition of bacon adds a salty contrast. Roasting brings out the sweetness of the vegetables and retains all the goodness.

1 eggplant (aubergine), cut into eight pieces lengthwise
3 orange sweet potatoes, peeled and cut into eight pieces lengthwise
3 parsnips, quartered lengthwise
150 g (5 oz) baby leeks, white part only, trimmed
2 tablespoons olive oil
2 tablespoons chopped fresh thyme or 2 teaspoons dried thyme
freshly ground black pepper
2 firm pears, cored and quartered
8 bacon slices, rind removed
1 tablespoon balsamic vinegar

Serves 4
Preparation 20 minutes
Cooking 50 minutes

1 Preheat the oven to 200°C (400°F/Gas 6). Arrange the eggplant, sweet potatoes, parsnips and leeks in a single layer in a wide roasting pan. Use a pastry brush to coat them lightly with the olive oil.

2 Sprinkle the thyme over the vegetables and season with black pepper. Bake for 25–30 minutes, until the vegetables are almost tender. Add the pear wedges, turning to lightly coat all the vegetables in the oil. Arrange the bacon slices over the vegetables.

3 Roast for another 15–20 minutes, until the vegetables and pears are tender and the bacon is lightly browned. Drizzle the vinegar over the roast vegetables and serve.

Cook's tip

If you arrange all the vegetables parallel in the roasting pan, they are easier and quicker to brush with oil.

Roasted potatoes and root vegetables

Root vegetables are at their peak in late autumn and winter; store them in the vegetable crisper in the fridge. Floury potatoes roast beautifully due to their high starch content.

4 roasting (floury) potatoes, such as desiree or pontiac
3 carrots
3 parsnips
3 small swedes (rutabaga) or turnips
olive oil, for drizzling
salt and freshly ground black pepper

Serves 6
Preparation 10 minutes
Cooking 45 minutes

1 Preheat the oven to 210°C (415°F/Gas 6–7). Wash and scrub all the vegetables, then pat dry with paper towels. Peel the potatoes and cut each in half.

2 Top and tail the carrots and parsnips, then cut them in half horizontally. Peel the swedes or turnips and cut into quarters.

3 Place all the vegetables in a large roasting pan, add a good splash of olive oil and season well with salt and black pepper. Roast for 30 minutes, then turn the vegetables and roast for another 15 minutes, or until golden and tender. Serve hot.

Cook's tip

To ensure that the potatoes will be crisp when cooked, it is essential to dry them thoroughly.

Cauliflower and broccoli gratin

Boosted with super-healthy broccoli and topped with crunchy walnuts, this fresh twist on an old favourite makes a great side dish, but is just as good on its own. Crunchy walnuts on top make this mouth-wateringly good.

melted butter, for brushing
1 large cauliflower, cut into florets
500 g (1 lb) broccoli, cut into florets
3 spring onions (scallions), sliced
¼ cup (30 g/1 oz) cornflour (cornstarch)
550 ml (19 fl oz) milk
⅔ cup (85 g/3 oz) grated mature cheddar or gruyère
1 egg, beaten
1⅔ cups (135 g/4½ oz) fresh breadcrumbs
freshly ground black pepper
¼ cup (30 g/1 oz) chopped walnuts

Serves 4
Preparation 20 minutes
Cooking 35 minutes

1 Preheat the oven to 190°C (375°F/Gas 5). Brush a baking dish or gratin dish with melted butter. Blanch the cauliflower and broccoli florets in a large saucepan of boiling water for 1 minute, then drain thoroughly and set aside.

2 Put the spring onions in the same saucepan the cauliflower and broccoli were blanched in. In a large heatproof bowl, mix the cornflour with a little of the milk to make a smooth paste. Pour the remaining milk into the saucepan with the spring onions and bring to a boil. Stir half the hot milk into the cornflour paste, mix well, then return the entire mixture to the saucepan. Bring to a boil, stirring frequently, to make a smooth white sauce.

3 Remove the sauce from the heat and stir in the cheese, egg and half the breadcrumbs. Stir in the blanched vegetables and season to taste with black pepper.

4 Transfer the mixture to a baking dish. Scatter the rest of the breadcrumbs and the walnuts over the top, then bake for about 20 minutes, until golden. Serve immediately.

Cauliflower cheese

Smooth, rich and velvety, cauliflower cheese, a long-time favourite, is traditionally served as an accompaniment to roast beef and roast potatoes. It's also lovely with fish. The addition of tomato will enliven it with extra colour and flavour.

1 small cauliflower (about 800 g/1¾ lb), cut into florets
2 tablespoons butter
2 tablespoons plain (all-purpose) flour
1¼ cups (310 ml/11 fl oz) milk
½ cup (60 g/2 oz) grated cheddar
salt and ground white pepper
1 tomato, peeled, seeded and roughly chopped (optional)

Serves 6
Preparation 15 minutes
Cooking 15 minutes

1 Steam the cauliflower over a saucepan of boiling water for 5–7 minutes, or until just tender. Drain and arrange in a single layer in a heatproof serving dish.

2 Meanwhile, melt the butter in a small saucepan over medium heat until bubbling. Add the flour and stir over low heat for 1 minute.

3 Add the milk, a little at a time, stirring after each addition until smooth. Bring to a boil and simmer for 2 minutes, stirring occasionally. Remove from the heat and stir in the cheese. Season to taste with salt and white pepper. Add the tomato if using.

4 Pour the cheese sauce over the cauliflower. Place under a hot grill (broiler), at least 15 cm (6 inches) from the heat, and cook for about 5 minutes, or until the sauce is golden brown. Serve immediately.

Cook's tip

When buying cauliflower, look for firm, creamy-white florets that are tight and without brown speckles. Check the condition of the base of the stem. If it is dry and discoloured, the cauliflower is certainly past its best.

Baked desserts

Bread and butter pudding

A perfect dessert for after a roast. The homely appeal of bread baked in custard is timeless. In this version, fruit loaf is used for extra flavour and a frothy cider sauce adds an enticing tang.

2 cups (500 ml/16 fl oz) milk
1¼ cups (310 ml/11 fl oz) thick (double) cream
1 vanilla bean, split lengthwise
1 day-old light fruit loaf, cut into slices
⅓ cup (90 g/3 oz) unsalted butter, softened
⅓ cup (40 g/1½ oz) sultanas (golden raisins)
6 egg yolks
½ cup (115 g/4 oz) caster (superfine) sugar
1 tablespoon freshly grated nutmeg
¼ cup (55 g/2 oz) raw (demerara) or brown sugar

CIDER SAUCE
1 cup (230 g/8 oz) caster (superfine) sugar
6 egg yolks
1¼ cups (310 ml/11 fl oz) dry cider

Serves 6
Preparation 30 minutes + 50 minutes soaking
Cooking 50 minutes

1 Gently heat the milk and cream in a saucepan with the vanilla bean until almost boiling. Remove from the heat, cover and leave to infuse for 30 minutes. Meanwhile, spread each slice of fruit loaf liberally with butter and cut in half diagonally. Overlap the slices attractively in a buttered, shallow baking dish, scattering the sultanas over the pieces as you go. Whisk the egg yolks and caster sugar in a bowl until pale and creamy. Strain the infused milk and cream into the egg mixture and whisk well. Pour over the buttered bread and leave to soak for 20 minutes.

2 Meanwhile, preheat the oven to 180°C (350°F/Gas 4). Sprinkle the nutmeg and raw sugar evenly over the pudding and set the dish in a roasting pan. Pour in enough boiling water to come halfway up the side of the dish and bake for 45 minutes, or until the custard has just set and the top is golden and crisp.

3 About 15 minutes before the pudding is due to come out of the oven, start making the cider sauce. Put the sugar and egg yolks in a heatproof bowl and place snugly over a pan of barely simmering water, making sure that the bottom of the bowl does not touch the water. Whisk until the egg and sugar mixture is pale and creamy and the sugar has dissolved. Still whisking, slowly pour in the cider and continue to whisk for 5 minutes, or until the mixture froths up to a creamy mousse. Whisk for another 5–10 minutes, or until the sauce is light and foamy. Pour the sauce into a jug and serve immediately with the hot pudding.

Oaty crumble

Apples, blackberries and oats: who says desserts are always bad for you? Served with custard, cream or ice cream, this is bound to become a family favourite. Try it with other fruits, such as pears, plums or apricots.

CRUMBLE TOPPING
1 cup (150 g/5 oz) plain (all-purpose) flour
⅓ cup (90 g/3 oz) butter, softened
½ cup (50 g/1¾ oz) rolled (porridge) oats
¼ cup (25 g/1 oz) ground almonds
¼ cup (55 g/2 oz) caster (superfine) sugar

5 cooking apples, peeled, cored and sliced
½ cup (115 g/4 oz) caster (superfine) sugar
1 large banana
175 g (6 oz) blackberries (thawed, if frozen)

Serves 6
Preparation 35 minutes
Cooking 45 minutes

1 To make the crumble topping, sift the flour into a bowl and rub in the butter until the mixture resembles fine breadcrumbs. Stir in the oats, ground almonds and sugar.

2 Preheat the oven to 190°C (375°F/Gas 5). Put the apples in a saucepan with the sugar and ⅓ cup (80 ml/2½ fl oz) water. Cover and cook gently for 10 minutes, or until they begin to soften. Remove from the heat.

3 Peel and slice the banana and stir it into the apples. Stir in the blackberries, then transfer the mixture to a 5 cup (1.25 litre/44 fl oz) baking dish. Set the dish on a baking tray. Spoon the crumble mixture evenly over the fruit and press it down very lightly.

4 Bake for 30–35 minutes, or until the crumble is golden brown and the juices from the filling begin to bubble up.

Rice pudding

An old-fashioned favourite and perhaps the ultimate comfort food, creamy rice pudding can be served plain or topped with jam or fruit. This lovely dessert can laze in the oven for a couple of hours.

45 g (1½ oz) butter
½ cup (110 g/3½ oz) short-grain rice
½ cup (115 g/4 oz) caster (superfine) sugar
1¼ cups (310 ml/11 fl oz) pouring cream
2½ cups (625 ml/21 fl oz) milk
freshly grated nutmeg, for sprinkling

Serves 4
Preparation 5 minutes
Cooking 2–2¼ hours

1 Preheat the oven to 160°C (320°F/Gas 2–3) and grease a 5 cup (1.25 litre/44 fl oz) ovenproof dish lightly with a third of the butter. Put the rice and caster sugar in the prepared dish and stir in the cream and milk.

2 Cut the remaining butter into tiny pieces and float them on the surface of the pudding. Grate the nutmeg over the top and cook on the centre shelf of the oven for 2 hours, or until the top is golden brown and the pudding is just set.

3 Take care not to overcook as the pudding will become dry. Remove from the oven and serve while still hot.

Cook's tip

For a fruity rice pudding, try adding some sultanas or other dried fruit to the rice before cooking.

Baked custards

For a richer, more decadent custard, replace some of the milk with cream. You can also infuse the milk with a wide strip of lemon or orange zest while it is heating, but ensure the bitter white pith has been removed.

melted butter, for brushing
2½ cups (625 ml/21 fl oz) milk
4 eggs
½ cup (115 g/4 oz) caster (superfine) sugar
1 teaspoon vanilla extract
pinch of ground nutmeg

Serves 6
Preparation 10 minutes
Cooking 25 minutes

1 Preheat the oven to 180°C (350°F/Gas 4). Lightly brush six ¾ cup (180 ml/6 fl oz) ramekins with melted butter.

2 Heat the milk in a small saucepan over medium heat until almost boiling.

3 Meanwhile, whisk the eggs, sugar and vanilla in a large jug. Gradually add the hot milk, whisking constantly — don't whisk too vigorously though as you don't want lots of froth on top of the custard. Pour into the ramekins and sprinkle lightly with nutmeg.

4 Fold a clean tea towel (dish towel) and place in a large baking dish. Stand the ramekins on the tea towel and pour in enough boiling water to come halfway up the side of the ramekins.

5 Bake for 20 minutes, or until the custards are just set but still wobbly — the tip of a small sharp knife should come out clean. Carefully lift the ramekins from the baking dish. Serve warm, at room temperature, or chilled.

Cook's tip

If you prefer to make one large custard, use a 5 cup (1.25 litre/44 fl oz) baking dish and extend the cooking time to 30 minutes.

Little custard pots

Served with cherry compote, these easy baked custards are sure to be a hit. Take care not to overcook them — they should be just set when you take them out of the oven. This dessert can be prepared well ahead of serving.

600 ml (21 fl oz) milk
1 vanilla bean, split lengthwise
melted butter, for brushing
2 eggs, plus 2 egg yolks
2½ tablespoons caster (superfine) sugar
½ teaspoon cornflour (cornstarch)

CHERRY COMPOTE
2 tablespoons raw (demerara) sugar
500 g (1 lb) fresh cherries, pitted
2 teaspoons arrowroot

Serves 6
Preparation 15 minutes + 15 minutes infusing
Cooking 40 minutes

1 Gently heat the milk and vanilla bean in a saucepan until almost boiling. Remove from the heat, cover and set aside to infuse for 15 minutes. Preheat the oven to 160°C (320°F/Gas 3). Lightly brush six ½ cup (125 ml/4 fl oz) ramekins with melted butter. Put the eggs, egg yolks, sugar and cornflour in a bowl and lightly whisk together. Bring the milk back to boiling point, then discard the vanilla bean and pour the hot milk over the egg mixture, whisking all the time. Strain the mixture, then divide among the ramekins.

2 Set the ramekins in a roasting pan and pour enough hot water into the pan to come halfway up the side of the ramekins. Bake for 30–35 minutes, or until the custards are just set but still wobbly — the tip of a small sharp knife should come out clean. Carefully lift the ramekins from the roasting pan and place on a wire rack to cool. Once cold, chill until ready to serve.

3 For the cherry compote, put the sugar and 100 ml (3½ fl oz) water in a saucepan and heat gently until the sugar has dissolved. Bring to a boil, then reduce the heat and add the cherries. Cover and simmer gently for 4–5 minutes, stirring occasionally, until soft. Remove the cherries to a serving bowl using a slotted spoon, leaving the juices in the pan.

4 Mix the arrowroot to a paste with 1 tablespoon cold water. Stir into the cherry juices and simmer for 1 minute, stirring until thickened and clear. Allow to cool for a few minutes, then pour over the cherries. The compote can be served warm or at room temperature. To serve, spoon a little cherry compote over each custard pot, and serve the remaining compote in a bowl.

Baked jam roly-poly

Orange-flavoured pastry filled with jam and raspberries makes this a grown-up version of a favourite nursery treat. Serve with custard or cream for a deliciously simple dessert.

1 punnet (150 g/5 oz) fresh raspberries, or 1⅔ cups (225 g/8 oz) frozen raspberries
2 cups (300 g/10 oz) self-raising flour
¼ cup (55 g/2 oz) caster (superfine) sugar
½ teaspoon salt
¾ teaspoon ground cinnamon
125 g (4 oz) suet or vegetable shortening
finely grated zest and juice of 1 large orange
125 g (4 oz) raspberry jam
¼ cup (30 g/1 oz) slivered almonds, lightly toasted
custard or pouring cream, to serve

Serves 4
Preparation 20 minutes
Cooking 55 minutes

1 If using frozen raspberries, take them out of the freezer and allow to thaw. Preheat the oven to 200°C (400°F/Gas 6). Sift the flour into a bowl and stir in 1 tablespoon of the sugar. Mix in the salt, cinnamon, suet and orange zest and make a well in the centre. If necessary, add water to make the orange juice up to ¾ cup (180 ml/6 fl oz) and pour into the flour well. Mix to form a soft dough.

2 Turn the dough out onto a lightly floured surface and roll out to about 35 x 25 cm (14 x 10 inches). Spread evenly with the jam to within 1 cm (½ inch) of the edge. Reserve about 2 tablespoons of the best raspberries for decoration and scatter the rest over the jam.

3 Brush the edges of the dough with a little cold water, roll up from a narrow end and press the join firmly to seal. Wrap the roll in a sheet of baking (parchment) paper, pleating the paper along the length of the roll to allow for expansion. Wrap again in the same way in a pleated sheet of foil.

4 Place on a baking tray and bake for 40 minutes. Remove from the oven, open out the foil and baking paper and bake for a further 15 minutes, or until lightly browned. Remove from the oven and leave to stand for 5 minutes. Carefully lift the roly-poly onto a warm serving plate. Sprinkle with the remaining sugar, the almonds and reserved raspberries. Serve with custard or drizzled with cream.

Lemon delicious pudding

As it bakes, this aptly named pudding separates into a delicate lemon sponge on top and a tangy lemon sauce underneath. Heartwarmingly comforting, it is an old favourite and always a winner.

45 g (1½ oz) unsalted butter, softened, plus melted butter for brushing
¾ cup (170 g/6 oz) caster (superfine) sugar
2 teaspoons finely grated lemon zest
3 eggs, separated
¼ cup (35 g/1 oz) self-raising flour
1 cup (250 ml/8 fl oz) milk
¼ cup (60 ml/2 fl oz) strained lemon juice
icing (confectioners') sugar, for sprinkling
rose petals, to decorate (optional)
pouring cream, to serve

Serves 6
Preparation 15 minutes
Cooking 1 hour

1 Preheat the oven to 160°C (320°F/Gas 2–3). Brush six 1 cup (250 ml/8 fl oz) ramekins with melted butter.

2 In a bowl, beat the butter, sugar and lemon zest together using electric beaters until light and fluffy and almost white. Beat in the egg yolks, fold in the flour, then gently mix in the milk and lemon juice.

3 In a separate bowl, whisk the egg whites until they hold soft peaks. Carefully fold them into the butter mixture.

4 Spoon the batter into the ramekins and set them in a roasting pan. Pour boiling water into the roasting pan to come halfway up the side of the ramekins. Bake on the lower shelf of the oven for 1 hour, or until a cake skewer inserted into the cake topping comes out clean.

5 Sift some icing sugar over each pudding and decorate with the rose petals, if using. Serve the puddings hot or warm, with the cream passed separately.

Baked almond-stuffed peaches

Stuffing is a simple way of making baked fruit special. Here peaches are filled with a mixture of dried apricots, almonds and amaretti biscuits. Macaroons can be used instead of amaretti, but you won't need as many.

5 large ripe but firm peaches
10 dried apricot halves, finely chopped
6 amaretti biscuits, crumbled
2 teaspoons almond essence
1 tablespoon brandy
1 medium egg white
⅓ cup (50 g/1¾ oz) blanched almonds

Serves 8
Preparation 20 minutes
Cooking 40 minutes

1 Preheat the oven to 180°C (350°F/Gas 4). Cut the peaches in half and remove the stones. Arrange 8 of the halves, cut-side up, in a shallow baking dish. Set aside. Finely chop the remaining peach halves.

2 Combine the chopped peach with the dried apricots, crumbled amaretti, almond essence, brandy and egg white. Stir until thoroughly combined.

3 Heat a small heavy-based frying pan and dry-fry the almonds, turning and tossing, until they are lightly browned in spots. Remove and chop, in a food processor or by hand, to make a mixture of small chunks of nuts and ground nuts.

4 Add the chopped almonds to the fruit and amaretti mixture and mix well. Use the mixture to fill the hollows in the peach halves. Cover the baking dish with a tent of cooking foil.

5 Bake for 25–30 minutes, then remove the foil. Increase the oven temperature to 200°C (400°F /Gas 6) and bake for a further 5 minutes or until the nutty topping is lightly browned. Serve warm, or chill before serving, if preferred.

Sauces, stuffings and accompaniments

Sauces

Make the most of your roast with these delicious sauces. Use them over the meat, with the vegetables, or simply on the side. Apple and pork, mint and lamb, cranberry and turkey, horseradish and beef – all are perfect partners.

Apple sauce

750 g (1½ lb) cooking apples, peeled, cored and roughly chopped
1 tablespoon lemon juice
½ teaspoon ground cinnamon
½ cup (110 g/3½ oz) sugar
salt and freshly ground black pepper

Place the apples, lemon juice, cinnamon and 2 cups (500 ml/16 fl oz) water in a saucepan. Bring to a boil over high heat and cook, uncovered, for 20 minutes or until smooth, stirring occasionally. Add the sugar, stir well, and season with salt and black pepper. Reduce the heat to medium and cook for 5 minutes, stirring occasionally, until the sugar has dissolved. Remove from the heat and serve hot or at room temperature. Makes about 3 cups (750 ml/26 fl oz).

Cranberry sauce

2 cups (440 g/15 oz) sugar
500 g (1 lb) fresh or frozen cranberries

Put the sugar in a saucepan with 2 cups (500 ml/16 fl oz) water. Bring to a boil over high heat and cook, uncovered, for 5 minutes. Add the cranberries and boil for a further 5 minutes. Remove from the heat, allow to cool, then refrigerate and serve cold. Makes about 2 cups (500 ml/16 fl oz).

Apple sauce with ginger

500 g (1 lb) cooking apples, peeled, cored and chopped
2.5 cm (1 inch) piece fresh root ginger, finely chopped
2 tablespoons caster (superfine) sugar

Put the apples, ginger, sugar and 2 tablespoons water into a small saucepan. Cover and simmer, stirring occasionally, for 10 minutes or until pulpy. Remove from the heat and set aside until roast is ready. Makes about 2 cups (500 ml/16 fl oz).

Onion sauce

1½ tablespoons butter
2 onions, thinly sliced
1 clove garlic, crushed
1 tablespoon plain (all-purpose) flour
1 cup (250 ml/8 fl oz) beef stock
freshly ground black pepper

Melt the butter in a frying pan over low heat. Add the onion and garlic and cook, stirring occasionally, for 10 minutes, or until the onion starts to caramelise. Add the flour and cook, stirring, for 2–3 minutes. Gradually stir in the stock and bring to a boil, then reduce the heat to medium–low and simmer for 10 minutes, or until slightly thickened. Season with black pepper and serve. Makes about 1 cup (250 ml/8 fl oz).

Mustard sauce

1 tablespoon butter
1 tablespoon plain (all-purpose) flour
1 teaspoon dijon mustard
1 teaspoon hot English mustard
1 teaspoon mustard powder
1 cup (250 ml/8 fl oz) milk

Melt the butter in the top of a double boiler. Add the flour, mustards and mustard powder and stir until smooth. Cook, stirring, for 2 minutes, then remove from the heat. Warm the milk and gradually add it to the flour, stirring continuously. Return to the heat and whisk until boiling; reduce the heat and simmer for 5 minutes. Serve immediately, or cover the surface with plastic wrap to prevent a skin forming. Makes about 1 cup (250 ml/8 fl oz).

Cook's tip

To keep white sauces from lumping, have the liquid the same temperature as the roux. Heat the milk separately and add it to the roux gradually, whisking continuously.

Horseradish sauce

1¼ cups (300 g/10 oz) sour cream
2 tablespoons finely grated fresh horseradish
2 tablespoons pouring cream
1 tablespoon finely chopped fresh chives
salt and freshly ground black pepper

Combine the sour cream, horseradish, cream and chives in a bowl. Season to taste. Refrigerate until required. Makes 1½ cups (375 g/13 oz).

Mint sauce

1 cup (30 g/1 oz) fresh mint leaves, roughly torn
2 teaspoons caster (superfine) sugar
2 tablespoons vinegar (white wine or malt vinegar)

Combine the mint leaves and sugar in a glass jug or bowl. Pour the vinegar and ¼ cup (60 ml/2 fl oz) boiling water over and stir to combine. Serve immediately. Makes about 1 cup (250 ml/8 fl oz).

White sauce

1 tablespoon butter or margarine
1 tablespoon plain (all-purpose) flour
1 cup (250 ml/8 fl oz) hot milk
¼ teaspoon salt
pinch of ground white pepper

Melt the butter in a small heavy-based saucepan over low heat. Whisk in the flour, stirring constantly for 2–3 minutes until smooth. Gradually stir in the milk. Increase the heat to medium and cook, stirring constantly, for 3–5 minutes, until the sauce is thickened and smooth and no raw flour taste remains. Remove from the heat and stir in the salt and white pepper. If not using the sauce immediately, place a single layer of plastic wrap flat on the surface to keep a skin from forming. Cool to room temperature and refrigerate until needed; reheat in the top of a double boiler. Use as a base for other sauces. Makes 1 cup (250 ml/8 fl oz).

For 1 cup (250 ml/8 fl oz) white sauce

	Butter	Flour	Milk
Thin	1 tblspn	1 tblspn	1 cup
Medium	2 tblspns	2 tblspns	1 cup
Thick	3 tblspns	3 tblspns	1 cup

Stuffings

Stuffing lamb and leaner cuts of beef infuses the meat with extra flavour and helps the flesh stay juicy while the exterior slowly roasts in the hot oven. They're also a delicious treat to accompany the meat.

Fruity stuffing

SUITABLE FOR BEEF AND LAMB

1 cup (80 g/2½ oz) fresh breadcrumbs
½ cup (100 g/3½ oz) chopped dried apricots
¼ cup (35 g/1 oz) currants
3 tablespoons chopped fresh parsley
2 tablespoons butter, melted

Put all the ingredients in a bowl and mix together well. Sufficient for stuffing a 1.5 kg (3 lb) shoulder of lamb once it has been boned. Makes about 2 cups (275 g/9 oz)

Ricotta and herb stuffing

SUITABLE FOR BEEF AND LAMB

2 cups (500 g/1 lb) ricotta
½ cup (10 g/½ oz) fresh mint, roughly chopped
½ cup (10 g/½ oz) fresh flat-leaf parsley, roughly chopped
2 tablespoons fresh basil, roughly chopped
2 tablespoons fresh sage, roughly chopped
2 tablespoons fresh thyme, roughly chopped
1 egg
salt and freshly ground black pepper

Place the ricotta in a large bowl and mash with a fork until soft. Add the herbs and egg and season with a little salt and black pepper. Mix until well combined. Makes about 3½ cups (600 g/1 lb 5 oz)

Cook's tip

Replace the herbs with 1 tablespoon finely grated lemon zest, 4 tablespoons roughly chopped fresh oregano and 2 tablespoons roughly chopped chives.

Apple, walnut and prune

SUITABLE FOR POULTRY

⅓ cup (90 g/3 oz) chopped pitted prunes
¼ cup (60 ml/2 fl oz) port or fresh orange juice
1 small apple, cored and finely chopped
¼ cup (30 g/1 oz) walnut pieces, chopped
1 cup (80 g/2½ oz) fresh breadcrumbs
1–2 tablespoons fresh thyme
1 egg, beaten
salt and freshly ground black pepper

Put the prunes in a small saucepan and add the port. Set over low heat and bring almost to the boil so the prunes absorb the liquid, then tip into a bowl. Add the apple, walnuts, breadcrumbs, thyme, egg and seasoning and mix well. Stuff into the neck end of a chicken or turkey, shaping any leftover stuffing into walnut-sized balls to cook separately – bake them on a lightly oiled baking tray for the last 20 minutes of the bird's cooking time.

Cook's tip

You can also bake the entire stuffing mixture separately. Place in a greased 17.5 cm (7 inch) diameter baking dish, packing it down evenly. Bake at 200°C (400°F/Gas 6) for 40 minutes. Serves 6.

Sage, potato and onion

SUITABLE FOR POULTRY

1 kg (2 lb) all-purpose potatoes, peeled
¼ cup (60 ml/2 fl oz) vegetable oil
3 large brown (yellow) onions, chopped
⅓ cup (80 ml/2½ fl oz) milk
¾ teaspoon crumbled dried sage
¾ teaspoon salt
½ teaspoon freshly ground black pepper

Boil, steam or microwave the potatoes until tender, then drain well and place in a large bowl. Meanwhile, heat the oil in a saucepan over medium heat and sauté the onions for 5 minutes, until soft. Add the milk to the potatoes and lightly mash, then mix in the onions and remaining ingredients. Spoon loosely into the body cavity of the bird.

Sausage and chestnut

SUITABLE FOR POULTRY

100 g (3½ oz) good-quality pork sausages
100 g (3½ oz) cooked or vacuum-packed chestnuts, finely chopped (or use the same quantity of canned unsweetened chestnut purée)
2 French shallots, finely chopped
1 cup (80 g/2½ oz) fresh breadcrumbs
1½ tablespoons chopped fresh sage
1 egg, beaten
salt and freshly ground black pepper

Remove the sausage meat from the casings and place in a bowl. Mix in the chestnuts and shallots. Add the breadcrumbs, sage, egg and some seasoning and mix thoroughly. Stuff into the neck end of a chicken or turkey, shaping any leftover stuffing into walnut-sized balls to cook separately – bake them on a lightly oiled baking tray for the last 30 minutes of the bird's cooking time.

Cook's tip

For a simple sage and onion stuffing, sauté 3 chopped onions in 1½ tablespoons butter until soft and golden. Add 2 cups (160 g/5 oz) fresh breadcrumbs, 2 tablespoons chopped fresh sage or 2 teaspoons crumbled dried sage, 1 beaten egg and season to taste with salt and freshly ground black pepper.

Celery stuffing

SUITABLE FOR POULTRY

⅓ cup (90 g/3 oz) butter, softened
2 onions, chopped
4 stalks celery, chopped
275 g (9 oz) two-day-old wholemeal (wholewheat) bread, crusts removed, made into breadcrumbs
½ cup (60 g/2 oz) roughly chopped walnuts
2 tablespoons chopped fresh marjoram
4 tablespoons chopped fresh parsley
finely grated zest and strained juice of ½ orange
salt and freshly ground black pepper
1 egg, beaten

To make the stuffing, melt the butter in a large frying pan over low–medium heat. Sauté the onions and celery for 5 minutes, taking care they don't burn. Tip into a bowl, then add the breadcrumbs, walnuts, herbs, orange zest and juice. Season well with salt and black pepper, stir in the egg and leave to cool. Serves 6–8.

Cook's tip

Many herbs go beautifully with fish. Use any of the following to season a stuffing: fresh thyme and parsley; fresh basil, chervil, coriander (cilantro), dill; a bit of mint with parsley or dill; tarragon and sage.

Herb stuffing

SUITABLE FOR FISH

3 tablespoons chopped fresh parsley
3 tablespoons grated parmesan
1 cup (100 g/3½ oz) dry breadcrumbs
1 teaspoon dried thyme, crumbled
80 g (2½ oz) unsalted butter or margarine, melted
½ teaspoon salt
½ teaspoon freshly ground black pepper

Put all the ingredients in a bowl and mix together well. This amount of stuffing is sufficient for a 2 kg (4 lb) fish.

Mushroom stuffing

SUITABLE FOR FISH

100 g (3½ oz) mushrooms
1 French shallot
2 tablespoons fresh parsley
1 tablespoon butter
⅔ cup (55 g/2 oz) fresh breadcrumbs
salt and freshly ground black pepper
1 egg, beaten

Finely chop the mushrooms, shallot and parsley. Melt the butter in a frying pan over low–medium heat. Fry the mushrooms and shallot in the hot butter for a few minutes. Add the parsley, breadcrumbs, salt and black pepper and mix well, then moisten the mixture with a little of the beaten egg.

Left: To stuff a butterflied fish, first open the fish flat on a baking tray and then heap each side with stuffing. Bake the fish opened flat.

Gravies

A roast just isn't a roast unless there's a good gravy involved – all the juicy goodness from the meat distilled into a smooth sauce that adds extra savour. And so easy to do!

Au jus gravy

Drain all but 1 tablespoon of clear drippings from the roasting pan. Add 2 cups (500 ml/16 fl oz) beef stock, hot water or vegetable cooking water and place on the stovetop over medium heat, scraping up the browned bits. Cook for 3–4 minutes, until slightly reduced. Season with salt and freshly ground black pepper to taste. Makes 2 cups (500 ml/16 fl oz).

Beef gravy

Pour ¼ cup (60 ml/2 fl oz) roast beef drippings into a large frying pan (add some melted butter if you don't have quite enough); set aside. Place the roasting pan over medium heat, pour in 2 cups (500 ml/16 fl oz) beef stock, or 1 cup (250 ml/8 fl oz) stock and 1 cup (250 ml/8 fl oz) water. Simmer, scraping up the browned bits, for 1 minute. Place the frying pan over medium heat for 1 minute. Blend in ¼ cup (35 g/1 oz) flour and whisk for 1–2 minutes. Gradually stir in the stock from the roasting pan and whisk until the mixture boils and thickens. Reduce the heat to medium–low and simmer, stirring occasionally, for 2–3 minutes. Add salt and freshly ground black pepper to taste. Strain through a sieve, if desired, and transfer to a warm gravy boat or jug to serve. Makes 2 cups (500 ml/16 fl oz).

Traditional pan gravy

Remove the roasted meat from the roasting pan. Drain away the fat keeping about 1 tablespoon in the pan. Place the pan on the stovetop over medium heat. Bring to a boil. Add 4 tablespoons plain (all-purpose) flour and stir until combined. Reduce the heat and cook, stirring often until the flour mixture is well browned. Remove the pan from the heat and slowly pour in 3½ cups (875 ml/30 fl oz) beef stock, stirring constantly until well combined. Return the pan to the heat, bring mixture to a boil. Reduce heat and simmer for about 3 minutes, stirring occasionally. Season with salt and freshly ground black pepper.

Chicken gravy

Skim the fat from the roasting pan juices. Place the roasting pan on the stovetop and bring the pan juices to a boil. Add 150 ml (5 fl oz) dry white wine and bring back to a boil, scraping up all the browned bits from the bottom of the pan. Boil for 1 minute and season to taste with salt and freshly ground black pepper. If the gravy looks too thin, drain off a few tablespoons of the gravy, stir in 1 tablespoon plain (all-purpose) flour until well blended, then stir the mixture back into the gravy and cook, stirring, for several minutes, or until the gravy has thickened.

Sides

Of course, there's vegetables and gravy, Yorkshire puddings (page 22) and comforting desserts, but you can add even more creative pizzazz to your roast dinner with these accompaniments.

Pickled onions

Put 500 g (1 lb) small pickling onions in boiling water for 2–3 minutes, remove when soft and peel. Cover with 60 g (2 oz) salt and set aside for 24 hours. In a saucepan over low–medium heat, add 2 cups (500 ml/16 fl oz) malt vinegar, ¼ cup (55 g/2 oz) sugar, 6 cloves, 6 black peppercorns and 1 tablespoon pickling spice and heat until the sugar melts. Add the onions and boil for 5 minutes.

Place the onions in a sterilised jar and cover with the vinegar mixture. Top with a fresh red chilli. Seal the jar. The onions will be ready for eating in about 2 weeks. Makes 500 g (1 lb).

Tzatziki

In a medium bowl, combine 1 tablespoon olive oil and 2 teaspoons lemon juice. Fold 2 cups (500 g/1 lb) Greek-style yogurt in slowly, making sure it mixes completely with the oil. Add 8 cloves finely chopped garlic and ½ cup grated cucumber. Stir until evenly distributed. Makes about 2½ cups (750 g/1 lb10 oz).

Tomato chutney

Chop 500 g (1 lb) green tomatoes, peel, core and chop 500 g (1 lb) granny smith apples and peel and chop 500 g (1 lb) onions. Place in a bowl, stir, cover and set aside in a cool spot for about 12 hours. In a large saucepan over medium heat, put 1 seeded and sliced chilli, 2 tablespoons freshly grated nutmeg, 60 g (2 oz) sultanas, 175 g (6 oz) brown sugar, 300 ml (10 fl oz) malt vinegar, 3 tablespoons honey, 2 tablespoons cloves, 60 g (2 oz) raisins and ¼ teaspoon cayenne pepper and bring to a boil. Reduce the heat and cook gently for 2 hours, stirring often. Spoon into sterilised jars and seal. Makes about 1 kg (2 lb).

Cook's tip

Tzatziki is a yogurt, cucumber and garlic dip traditionally served as an accompaniment to roast lamb in Greece. Adjust the amount of garlic to suit your taste.

Glazes

Glazes add an attractive sheen to food during cooking. They are typically quite sweet, subtly enhancing the flavour of food and sometimes adding a slight stickiness as they caramelise.

Apricot-ginger glaze

⅓ cup (80 ml/2½ fl oz) chicken stock
½ cup (160 g/5½ oz) apricot jam
1 tablespoon very finely chopped fresh ginger
¼ teaspoon freshly ground black pepper

Combine the ingredients in a small saucepan and mix well. Bring to a boil over medium heat, then reduce the heat to low and cook, stirring, for about 2 minutes, until well blended. Makes about 1 cup (250 ml/8 fl oz)

Honey-mustard glaze

⅓ cup (80 ml/2½ fl oz) chicken stock
2 tablespoons honey
2 tablespoons dijon mustard
½ teaspoon grated lemon zest

Combine the ingredients in a small saucepan and mix well. Bring to a boil over medium heat, then reduce the heat to low and cook, stirring, for about 2 minutes, until well blended.

Quince glaze

100 g (3½ oz) quince paste
¼ cup (60 ml/2 fl oz) red wine
1 tablespoon wholegrain mustard

Combine the ingredients in a small saucepan. Add ½ cup (125 ml/4 fl oz) water and whisk together over medium–low heat until smooth. Bring to a simmer and cook for 3 minutes, or until the mixture thickens.

Orange and wasabi glaze

1 cup (250 ml/8 fl oz) orange juice
½ cup (110 g/3½ oz) sugar
2 teaspoons fish sauce
1 tablespoon wasabi paste
1 tablespoon grated orange zest

Combine the orange juice and sugar in a saucepan. Bring to a boil over high heat, stirring frequently to dissolve the sugar. Reduce the heat to medium and cook for about 3 minutes, stirring occasionally, until the mixture thickens slightly. Remove from the heat and stir in the fish sauce, wasabi and orange zest.

Plum glaze

⅓ cup (80 ml/2½ fl oz) chicken stock
½ cup (125 ml/4 fl oz) plum sauce or plum preserve
3 tablespoons finely chopped spring onions (scallions)
1 tablespoon cider vinegar

Combine the ingredients in a small saucepan and mix well. Bring to a boil over medium heat, then reduce the heat to low and cook, stirring, for about 2 minutes, until well blended.

Fig glaze

½ cup (125 ml/4 fl oz) apple juice
1 cup (185 g/6½ oz) soft brown sugar
⅓ cup (100 g/3½ oz) fig jam
¼ teaspoon ground mixed spice
¼ teaspoon ground cinnamon

Combine the apple juice and sugar in a medium saucepan. Bring to a boil over high heat, stirring frequently to dissolve the sugar. Reduce the heat to medium and add the jam, mixed spice and cinnamon. Cook for about 3 minutes, stirring occasionally, until the mixture thickens slightly then remove from the heat.

Cook's tip

Brush the glaze on your chosen meat two or three times during the last 15–20 minutes of cooking.

Lime and mustard glaze

¼ cup (60 ml/2 fl oz) lime juice
1 cup (170 g/6 oz) soft brown sugar
⅓ cup (100 g/3½ oz) lime marmalade
⅓ cup (90 g/3 oz) mustard, such as dijon
1 tablespoon olive oil
¼ teaspoon ground cinnamon
¼ teaspoon ground cloves
1 tablespoon grated lime zest
salt and freshly ground black pepper

Combine the lime juice and sugar in a saucepan. Bring to a boil over high heat, stirring frequently to dissolve the sugar. Reduce the heat to medium and stir in the marmalade, mustard, olive oil, cinnamon and cloves. Cook for about 3 minutes, stirring occasionally, until the mixture thickens slightly. Stir in the lime zest and season with salt and black pepper.

Rubs and marinades

Homemade rubs and marinades enrich the flavour and aroma of meat, chicken, fish or vegetables, particularly when roasting. Add an exotic edge to your roast dinner with these flavourful suggestions.

Cajun rub

2 tablespoons paprika
1 tablespoon dried red chilli flakes
1 tablespoon celery salt
1 teaspoon allspice
2 cloves garlic
2 tablespoons dried onion flakes
2 tablespoons dried oregano
2 tablespoons dried thyme
1 teaspoon peppercorns

Using a pestle, pound all the ingredients in a mortar until fine and well combined. Store in an airtight container in the refrigerator for up to 1 month. Makes about 1 cup (140 g/5 oz).

Moroccan rub

1 teaspoon saffron threads
1 teaspoon harissa
1 teaspoon ground cardamom
4 cloves
1 teaspoon cumin seeds
2 cloves garlic
3 tablespoons fresh mint
3 tablespoons fresh coriander (cilantro) leaves

Using a pestle, pound all the ingredients in a mortar until fine and well combined. Store in an airtight container in the refrigerator for up to 1 month. Makes about ½ cup (70 g/2½ oz).

Greek rub

2 teaspoons dried oregano
1 teaspoon onion powder
1 teaspoon garlic powder
1 teaspoon salt
1 teaspoon cornflour (cornstarch)
1 teaspoon freshly ground black pepper
1 teaspoon dried parsley flakes
½ teaspoon ground cinnamon
½ teaspoon ground nutmeg

Combine all the ingredients and store in an airtight container. Keep in a cool, dark place. Makes about ½ cup (70 g/2½ oz).

Jamaican jerk seasoning

½ cup (50 g/1¾ oz) ground allspice berries
1 cup (185 g/6½ oz) soft brown sugar
6 cloves garlic
4 Scotch bonnet chillies (a variety of habañero and very hot)
1 tablespoon dried thyme or 2 tablespoons fresh thyme
8 spring onions (scallions), chopped
1 teaspoon ground cinnamon
½ teaspoon ground nutmeg
salt and freshly ground black pepper, to taste
2 tablespoons soy sauce

Place all the ingredients in a food processor and blend to a paste. Store in an airtight container in the refrigerator for up to 1 month. Makes about 2 cups (275 g/9 oz).

Spice rub

2 tablespoons salt
2 tablespoons soft brown sugar
2 tablespoons ground cumin
2 tablespoons chilli powder
2 tablespoons freshly ground black pepper
1 tablespoon cayenne pepper
3 tablespoons paprika

Combine all the ingredients and store in an airtight container in the refrigerator for up to 1 month. Use on beef, chicken, lamb or pork. Makes about 1 cup (140 g/5 oz).

Mediterranean rub

1 tablespoon dried oregano
1 tablespoon dried marjoram
1 tablespoon dried parsley
1 tablespoon dried basil
1 teaspoon sea salt
½ teaspoon black peppercorns
2 cloves garlic, roughly chopped
1 tablespoon grated lemon zest

Using a pestle, pound all the ingredients in a mortar until fine and well combined. Store in an airtight container in the refrigerator for up to 1 month. Makes about 1 cup (140 g/5 oz).

Classic herb marinade

½ cup (125 ml/4 fl oz) balsamic vinegar
½ cup (125 ml/4 fl oz) olive oil
3 tablespoons chopped fresh parsley or coriander (cilantro)
2 tablespoons finely chopped fresh dill
½ teaspoon salt
pinch of freshly ground black pepper

Place the ingredients in a screw-top jar. Shake well to combine. Makes 1½ cups (200 g/7 oz).

Beef marinade

¾ cup (180 ml/6 fl oz) olive oil
2 tablespoons worcestershire sauce
2 tablespoons lemon juice
6 tablespoons soy sauce
4 tablespoons wine vinegar
salt and freshly ground black pepper

Mix and put over roast. Let marinate overnight. Makes about 1 cup (250 ml/8 fl oz).

INDEX

ROAST DINNER
Copy Editors Katri Hilden, Emma Hutchinson
Designer Jacqueline Duncan
Proofreader Susin Chow
Indexer Diane Harriman
Senior Production Controller Monique Tesoriero
Editorial Project Manager Deborah Nixon

READER'S DIGEST GENERAL BOOKS
Editorial Director Elaine Russell
Managing Editor Rosemary McDonald
Art Director Carole Orbell

Roast Dinner is published by
Reader's Digest (Australia) Pty Limited
80 Bay Street, Ultimo NSW 2007
www.readersdigest.com.au
www.readersdigest.co.nz
www.readersdigest.co.za

First published 2010. Reprinted 2010.

National Library of Australia Cataloguing-in-Publication entry

Title: Roast dinner.
ISBN: 978-1-921569-81-4 (pbk)
Notes: Includes index.
Subjects: Roasting (Cookery)
Other Authors: Reader's Digest (Australia)
Dewey Number: 641.71

Prepress by Sinnott Bros, Sydney
Printed and bound by Leo Paper Products, China

We are interested in receiving your comments on the contents of this book. Write to: The Editor, General Books Editorial, Reader's Digest (Australia) Pty Limited, GPO Box 4353, Sydney, NSW 2001, or email us at bookeditors.au@readersdigest.com

To order additional copies of *Roast Dinner,* please contact us as follows:
www.readersdigest.com.au, 1300 300 030 (Australia);
www.readersdigest.co.nz, 0800 400 060 (New Zealand);
www.readersdigest.co.za, 0800 980 572 (South Africa)
or email us at customerservice@readersdigest.com.au

Roast Dinner contains material first published in the following Reader's Digest books: *Cook Smart for a Healthy Heart*, *The Complete Book of Herbs*, *Eat Yourself Healthy*, *Good Food for Less*, *The Great Potato Cookbook*, *Healthy One-Dish Cooking*, *Kitchen Secrets*, *Like Grandma Used to Make*, *Your Cooking Questions Answered*, and *Eggs, Milk & Cheese*, *Meat Classics* and *Perfect Poultry* from the Eat Well Live Well series.

Front cover photograph: Roast leg of lamb with rosemary, page 38

A note on weights and measures

Sometimes conversions within a recipe are not exact but are the closest conversion that is a suitable measurement for each system. Use either the metric or the imperial measurements; do not mix the two systems.

All cup and spoon measurements are level unless stated otherwise.

Product code 041-4045